Samuel Richardson

Twayne's English Authors Series

Bertram H. Davis, Editor

Florida State University

TEAS 454

SAMUEL RICHARDSON
Portrait by J. Highmore, ca. 1747
Courtesy of the National Portrait Gallery, London

Samuel Richardson

By Elizabeth Bergen Brophy

College of New Rochelle

Twayne Publishers
A Division of G. K. Hall & Co. • Boston

Copyediting supervised by Lewis DeSimone
Book production by Kristina Hals
Book design by Barbara Anderson

Typeset in 11 pt Garamond
by Compset, Inc., of Beverly, Massachusetts

Printed on permanent/durable acid-free paper
and bound in the United States of America

Library of Congress Cataloging in Publication Data

Brophy, Elizabeth Bergen, 1929–
    Samuel Richardson.

    (Twayne's English authors series ; TEAS 454)
    Bibliography: p.
    Includes index.
    1. Richardson, Samuel, 1689–1761—Criticism and
interpretation. I. Title. II. Series.
PR3667.B68   1987   823'.6   87-2884
ISBN 0-8057-6951-X (alk. paper)

To
Sheila and Steve, David, Kate, Liz, and Jim,
who always help

Contents

About the Author

Elizabeth Bergen Brophy is professor of English at the College of New Rochelle. She received her B.A. from Smith College and her Ph.D. from Columbia University. She has held a Columbia Traveling Fellowship, a Fulbright Fellowship (England), an ACLS Fellowship, and a National Endowment for the Humanities Fellowship. Previous publications include *Samuel Richardson: The Triumph of Craft* (1974) as well as articles on eighteenth-century topics and modern satire.

Preface

This is a good time for Richardson scholars. Richardson's critical reputation today is perhaps as high as it has ever been. In his own age, while Diderot placed him on a plane with the Bible and Homer, detractors questioned both his moral vision and his artistry. Controversy over the novels has by no means been stilled, but critics of almost every persuasion—historical, mythic, sociological, textual, Marxist, feminist, deconstructionist—join in finding much to say about Richardson, and usually much to admire.

In this study I have aimed at providing an accessible guide to those who are relative newcomers to Richardson's novels. I have therefore presented a somewhat conventional overview of Richardson's life and work, addressing the standard cruxes that are raised in assessing the novels, such as the nature of Pamela's virtue and the degree of villainy evidenced by Mr. B., Clarissa's imputed sexual frigidity and the problem of Lovelace's appeal for readers, Harriet Byron's assertiveness and Sir Charles's perhaps too constant virtue. I have also, however, argued against the commonly held position that Richardson was very much a man of his age who passively, and even unconsciously, reflected the values of his own time. On the contrary, I hold that Richardson was a radical social critic who found the codes of his society immoral and destructive.

Clarissa is a great novel because of its sophisticated literary techniques and its unparalleled psychological penetration, but it is also a scathing, revolutionary indictment of many of the implicit standards of the polite eighteenth-century world. Clarissa and Lovelace are both tragic figures, persons with a potential for greatness who have been destroyed by a vicious system of values. In the Harlowe family we see the venal insensitiveness of "respectable" codes, while in Lovelace we see the arid futility of the code of the rake. *Sir Charles Grandison* is best understood not, as so many have implied, as a clumsy attempt to present the manners of high society but rather as a utopian portrait of a new ideal. The depiction of perfection is notoriously difficult, and the novel does not escape all of the hazards intrinsic to such a project, but its strengths and weaknesses can be better understood in their proper context. *Pamela,* Richardson's first novel, perhaps comes closest to simply reflecting the realities of its age, but its happy ending is only possible because Mr. B. does see the error of his ways, and does continue to change through his acknowledgment of Pamela's real superiority. Unlike Lovelace, Mr. B. has not been irretrievably distorted by false values. Happiness for the couple finally results not from following the conduct book rules, but by creating a different model of companionate marriage. New values emerge when Richardson's work is seen in this perspective—that of his vehement and deliberate denunciation of the most pervasive values of his own culture.

I would like to thank the National Portrait Gallery for permission to use Joseph Highmore's portrait of Richardson as a frontispiece. I also thank the many efficient and courteous people who helped me at the British Library, the library of the Victoria and Albert Museum, the Bodleian, the Berg Collection of the New York Public Library, the Beinecke Library of Yale University, the Pierpont Morgan Library, and, last but not least, the librarians of the College of New Rochelle. I am grateful to Professor Bertram Davis who has encouraged me in writing this work and to Professor John Middendorf who first suggested my writing it.

As always, my largest debt is to my husband for his intelligent comments and for his unfailing support. I also thank my daughter, Sheila Peiffer, for her accurate and tactful typing.

Elizabeth Bergen Brophy

College of New Rochelle

Chronology

Chapter One
Life and Minor Works

Samuel Richardson was, in the best Horatio Alger tradition, a self-made man. He rose from relative poverty to become a highly successful business man, as well as the official printer for the House of Commons and the printer of the *Philosophical Transactions* for the Royal Society. He was honored by his peers in his election as Master of the Stationers' Company. This financial success was accomplished without any taint of sharp dealing or unethical practice, and, indeed, as William Sale, Jr., has pointed out,[1] Richardson's treatment of his apprentices was exemplary for his time and led to many of them advancing in their profession after leaving his employment. All the evidence indicates that he was himself the "good man" that his writings praised.

Information about Richardson's early life is largely based on an account he wrote himself for the use of his Dutch translator, Johannes Stinstra. This has now been expanded by the researches of T. C. Duncan Eaves and Ben D. Kimpel in their authoritative biography, *Samuel Richardson.*[2] He was born in Derbyshire, and baptized in the Mackworth parish church in 1689. For reasons that are obscure (Richardson hints at political persecution, but Eaves and Kimpel cast doubt on this),[3] his father, a joiner by trade, had left London but returned to it about 1700, when Richardson would have been eleven years old. Richardson, in his letters to Stinstra,[4] reports that he wished to be a clergyman but that his father, unable to support him in gaining the necessary education (Richardson was one of nine children), gave him the freedom to choose a business. He had "only common School-Learning,"[5] he writes, and he chose to be bound apprentice to a printer because "I thought it would gratify my Thirst after Reading."[6] He was bound apprentice to John Wilde in 1706[7] and, by his own account, "served a diligent seven years to it, to a Master who grudged every Hour to me, that tended not to his profits"; "I took care that even my Candle was of my own purchasing that I might not in the most trifling Instance make my Master a Sufferer."[8]

Richardson completed his apprenticeship, worked as a journeyman, and soon set up in business for himself, marrying Martha Wilde, the daughter of his employer, who brought him the modest dowry of £100.[9] The marriage seems to have been a happy and companionable one, saddened by the early deaths of their six children, five sons and one daughter, none of whom lived to be more than three. Richardson wrote in 1748, "I cherish the Memory of my lost Wife to this hour," adding, "I assure you that I can do so without derogating from the Merits of, or being disallowed by my present; who speaks of her on all Occasions as respectfully, and as affectionately, as I do myself."[10] Shortly after the death of his last child, Richardson, a widower for two years, married Elizabeth Leake, whose brother was a bookseller in Bath. Again, the marriage seems to have been happy. Six children were born to this marriage, but while two, Elizabeth and Samuel, also died when less than a year of age, four daughters, Mary (Polly), Martha (Patty), Anne (Nancy), and Sarah (Sally), survived. Richardson, like his hero Sir Charles Grandison, preferred to spend his leisure time with his own family, and his wife was the first audience for *Pamela*. Letters hint at a few domestic rubs. For example, when Richardson moved both his home and his business to his final residence, 11 Salisbury Square, he commented, "Everybody is more pleased with what I have done than my Wife."[11] But on the whole, they seem to have typified what Richardson himself felt to be the ideal in marriage: where "love is but the harbinger to . . . friendship; and that friendship therefore is the perfection of love, and superior to love; it is love purified, exalted, proved by experience and a consent of minds."[12] Richardson usually denigrated mere "romantic love" as a "blazing, crackling, green-wood flame, as much smoke as flame,"[13] but in a letter to Lady Bradshaugh he did recount a mysterious early passion. After describing various unsatisfactory proposals of marriage made to him in his youth—a pretty idiot, a violent Roman Catholic, a gay, high-spirited, volatile lady—he then confesses, "Another there was whom his soul loved; but with a reverence—Hush!—Pen, lie thee down!—."[14] This lady may have been the Mrs. Beaumont whose narrative Richardson once began and then abandoned,[15] and who later appears as a minor character in *Sir Charles Grandison.*

Richardson's life, which followed the ethical and moral principles that he advocated in his writings, led R. F. Brissenden to declare, in 1958, that "The character of Richardson is an affront to every conception of what an artist should be,"[16] and it seems true that some hazy postromantic conception of what constitutes the "artistic temperament" has resulted in a tendency to patronize Richardson as a writer. Boswell, who disliked both Richardson and his works, enjoyed relaying Johnson's remarks on Richardson's love of praise, but he was also honest enough to record Johnson's unequivocal preference for Richardson's novels over Fielding's.[17]

Much has been made of Richardson's friendships with women. If, indeed, this should be considered a failing at all, it ought to be noted that they were women of intelligence and spirit whom Richardson encouraged to engage in lively debate not only on his own works but also on moral and ethical topics. Elizabeth Carter and Hester Mulso were also admired by Johnson while Mary Delany and Ann Donnellan won the praise of Swift. Furthermore, Richardson did have lasting friendships with Edward Young, Aaron Hill, and Thomas Edwards, all literary figures and scholars, as well as with Johnson himself. Onslow, the speaker of the House of Commons was a warm friend, as well as colleagues in the printing business. It was to Richardson that Johnson turned when imprisoned for debt, and Johnson was a frequent caller at Richardson's house, citing him to Boswell as one of the few men he would take the trouble to seek after.[18] In 1753 Hogarth first met Johnson in Richardson's parlor, and was so taken aback by Johnson's physical mannerisms that he thought this stranger was "an idiot, whom his relations had put under the care of Mr. Richardson, as a very good man."[19] The anecdote tells us not only of the friendship between the two men but of Richardson's known and deserved reputation as a charitable man. Johnson, of only four *Ramblers* not written by himself, requested one from Richardson, and Richardson's works are quoted far more frequently in the *Dictionary* than any other contemporary author—*Clarissa* is cited ninety-seven times and *Pamela* three.[20]

It is certainly true that Richardson was a diffident man, conscious both of his lack of a traditional classical education and of his middle-class origin and status. He was also troubled in the last decades of his life with a "nervous complaint," most probably Parkinson's disease[21] that made him avoid crowds. However, he was also proud of his independence and of his well-earned position, despite joking references to living on "the wrong side of Temple Bar" (i.e., the city, rather than the fashionable West End). In his writings he deplored the denigration of businessmen and the depreciation of those not learned in the classics.

Why did this middle-aged, prosperous printer turn novelist? Richardson recounts to Stinstra that "From my earliest Youth, I had a Love of Letter-writing."[22] He tells of a correspondence with a gentleman greatly his superior in degree who "was a Master of the Epistolary Style" and of writing anonymously, when he was only eleven, to chide a neighborhood busybody. He also records that at the age of thirteen he was used as a letter writer by three young women of his acquaintance to write to their suitors. At school, his schoolmates "delighted to single me out," he notes, "to tell them Stories as they phrased it."[23] Some he had learned from reading, but others were of his own invention.

The immediate occasion for Richardson's writing of *Pamela* was his being asked by two publishers, Osborn and Rivington, to write a book of familiar letters. He had evidently become known in the trade through, he tells Stinstra, "the Readiness I shewed to oblige them, with writing Indexes, Prefaces, and sometimes, for their minor Authors, *honest* Dedications; abstracting, abridging, compiling, and giving my Opinion of Pieces offered them."[24] Some of the minor works which would be known to publishers, all issued anonymously except for the last named, were *The Apprentice's Vade Mecum: or, Young Man's Pocket-Companion* (1733), *A Seasonable Examination of the Pleas and Pretensions of the Proprietors of and Subscribers to, Play-Houses* (1733), his revisions of Defoe's *The Complete English Tradesman* (1737) and *A Tour thro' the Whole Island of Great Britain* (1738),[25] his revision for children of L'Estrange's translation of *Aesop's Fables* (1739), and his ambitious chapter headings for *The Negotiations of Sir Thomas Roe* (1740).

The Apprentice's Vade Mecum was adapted from a letter Richardson had written to his nephew, Thomas Richardson, who was apprenticed to his uncle in 1732. Fearing that the boy might take advantage of their relationship, he wrote a long letter setting forth the rules and regulations by which all apprentices were to abide. The tone of the letter is just what one would expect: the apprentice is to be hard working, respectful, and virtuous. Richardson also shows the benevolent side of his character when he cautions his nephew not to give pain to others, and to detest bad actions without scorning the sinner. The published pamphlet expands upon these ideas and removes all personal references. The tone is that of genuine concern for the future career of the young man himself, not merely assuring good value for the employer. Part 1 explains the apprentice's indentures, and also condemns gaming, fornication, taverns, and playhouses. One of Richardson's chief reasons for condemning the theater, at a low ebb in the early eighteenth century, was not merely its frivolity or immorality but the tendency of dramatists to make fun of "citizens" upon whom, in Richardson's opinion, the support of the nation relied. Part 2 is the original letter, revised, and part 3 is a condemnation of deism, which supports no specific church but emphasizes the primacy of Christian revelation.

A Seasonable Examination is less surely attributed to Richardson, but in the opinion of both McKillop and Eaves and Kimpel was probably his work.[26] It supports a bill that would limit the number of playhouses and regulate them to prevent offences against piety and decorum. In condemning the general moral tone of contemporary drama, it again stresses that most plays are written from the viewpoint of the upper classes and therefore are harmful in tending to make the youth of the middle or lower classes discontented by showing them an unattainable style of life, and also in mocking the middle-class tradesman, who is, in fact, the basis of England's prosperity.

Richardson's revisions of Defoe's works were designed chiefly to bring the volumes up to date, but he also shifted the emphasis of the *Tour* by including more information on cultural landmarks, such as ancient monuments and country seats, rather than purely economic commentary on agriculture and manufacturing. He tended to alter the work as well from first-person observation to an impartial reference work based upon information rather than personal experience. This was only logical, since Richardson was certainly no traveler, seldom venturing farther than his summer house in Fulham. While Defoe's interest in commerce and trading remains predominant, attention is now given to the details of town governments, and to places of minor economic importance such as Cambridge, the Isle of Wight, and the highlands and western isles of Scotland.

Richardson himself acknowledged his identity as the reviser of L'Estrange's *Aesop's Fables* in his letter to Stinstra, and sent Stinstra a copy of the book. In this work Richardson shortened L'Estrange's *Fables,* including only 240 whereas L'Estrange had originally used 500. He was determined to keep politics out of the work, but he did change L'Estrange's bias by either omitting or altering tales that supported monarchy and condemned popular government. He also tended to give a more serious turn to many of the stories, and to omit L'Estrange's occasional apparent admiration of clever trickery.[27] Sexually suggestive humorous anecdotes were cut. The morals or the reflections on the morals echo many of Richardson's known opinions: respect should be taught to children, belief in the afterlife is all-important, pride is a failing, the prosperous should be generous since they never know what fate may bring, good natures are better controlled by love than severity. Eaves and Kimpel comment, "The tendency of Richardson's fables, as indeed of fables in general, is a blend of practicality and morality, benevolence tempered with a proper regard for self."[28] Richardson's version does exhibit less cynicism than L'Estrange's, changing his conclusion of "Two Friends and a Bear" from "Every Man for Himself" to "Friendship is tried by Adversity," and suggesting that bad customs can debase men rather than that men are intrinsically evil. Apparently Richardson regarded the revision more as a useful contribution to the stock of books for children than as a literary achievement, since despite his acknowledgment to Stinstra, he seldom later referred to his authorship.

Still more of a labor of love was Richardson's work editing the *Negotiations of Sir Thomas Roe*. This was a series of letters written by Roe, a seventeenth-century statesman who served as British ambassador in Constantinople. Richardson thought the work deserved publication and persuaded the Society for the Advancement of Knowledge to oversee the editing, offering "to bear any part of the expense that shall be thought proper."[29] A committee was appointed to supervise the editing, and Richardson himself was asked to write the preface and a table of contents. His interpretation of the latter task went far beyond the usual format, amounting to a summary of the book, including cross references and explanations.[30] Apparently, both Richardson and the Society lost money on the volume, and the work was not continued. Richardson's energetic interpretation of his task certainly shows his unselfishness in promoting what he considered a worthy endeavor, and may perhaps indicate that the busy publisher was feeling an urge to write.

The *Familiar Letters* is the most important of Richardson's minor works. Not only did it lead directly to the composition of *Pamela,* but the letters themselves are interesting because they give insight into Richardson's beliefs, the moral and ethical concerns that inform his novels, and, in at least one instance, a glimpse of the style he would later develop. Richardson described to Stinstra the origin of this work: "Two Booksellers, my particular Friends, entreated me to write for them a little Volume of Letters, in a common Style, on such Subjects as might be of Use to those Country Readers who were unable to indite for themselves."[31] Such books of model letters as well as books on deportment were popular at the time, as they usually are in times of social mobility when those rising into a class of greater status need advice on how to act. Not uncharacteristically, Richardson immediately sought to exercise his own interests and concerns, asking the booksellers whether there would be "any Harm . . . in a Piece you want to be written so low, if we should instruct them how they should think and act in common Cases as well as indite?" The booksellers agreed and indeed, "They were the more urgent with me to begin the little Volume, for this Hint." Katherine Hornbeak, comparing Richardson's work with other collections of model letters, concludes that his volume is far more didactic than is usual. He omits the usual rules of form and stresses ethics rather than rhetoric, bringing his work closer to the domestic conduct books also popular at the time.[32] Some of the series of letters become little vignettes, proto-short stories, or character sketches rather than useful models for the semiliterate to emulate. Others, especially a series (letters 31–35) recommending servants, and a pair giving thanks for favors (114–15), are straightforward models notable for their brevity. Most are primarily expositions of proper modes of behavior as much as models of literary style.

One group can be classified as dealing with concerns of business and trade. These letters advocate, as one might expect, diligence and regularity as the key to success but, perhaps more unexpectedly, they also counsel forbearance and charity as not only virtuous but more effective than harsh measures. Letter 40, from an apprentice to his family, praises the kindness of his master and the "good order" to be found in the family so that "every servant, as well as I, knows his duty, and does it with pleasure."[33] His master, he writes, sees his diligence, and "puts me forward, and encourages me in such a manner, that I have great delight in it . . ." (46). In contrast, letter 51 tells of a master who spends more time at the tavern than at his affairs. The apprentice virtuously tries to help so that his family will not suffer, learning only to avoid these failings when his own time comes. Another letter (38) from an apprentice begs forgiveness for a "great misdemeanour." He writes to his master because he is afraid to brave his displeasure in person, and also so that his letter will "testify against me, if ever I willingly or knowingly offend again for the future"(45). He pleads that his master consider whether if his own children were to transgress he would not wish them to meet with "pardon rather than reprobation" and declares that "you may save a soul, as well as a body, from misery." The master shows mercy, responding that he will once more be lenient, and "hope for better, because I yet wish you well" (46). In letter 5 an apprentice seeks advice from his uncle. He has discovered a fellow apprentice in a breach of trust to their master and finds himself in a dilemma. "What must I do?," he writes, "If I discover the injury, I am sure to ruin a young man I would fain think possessed of some merit; if I conceal the injustice, I must at present share the guilt, and hereafter be partaker of the punishment" (11). His uncle advises him to tell his master immediately as "the only means of vindicating your own innocence" but also hopes that "the known clemency and good-nature of your master may pardon this offence." This forgiveness, he notes, ought to show the erring apprentice "the inhumanity of injuring a man . . . whose goodness deserves the best behaviour."

The same tone of Christian forbearance combined with a prudent concern with one's own welfare informs the letters which deal with relations between traders, and between tenants and landlords. Letter 102, from a town tenant to his landlord, pleads for more time to pay his rent, explaining unexpected disappointments in his trade, while letter 103, from a country tenant, similarly details a bad harvest and unhappy accidents "in a sick family, loss of cattle, etc." (132). The landlord replies, "I am unwilling to distress any *honest* man," but adds a note of caution: "I hope that I shall not meet with the *worse* usage for my forebearance: For *lenity* abused, even in generous tempers, provokes returns, that some people would call *severe*; but should not be deemed such if *just*" (133). Letter 105 satirizes a contrary approach. A steward writes to a tenant telling him that Sir John "is exceedingly provoked . . . and swears bloodily he'll seize, and throw you into gaol . . ." (133). The tenant's "moving answer" asks Sir John "if God Almighty, our common Landlord, should be *equally* hard upon us, what would become of us *all?*," and appeals to his self-interest by noting that if he is forced to sell his tools to raise the sum, "there is an end of *all*. I shall have no means left me then wherewith to pay his *honour,* or *anybody* else" (134). The steward replies that Sir John, moved by the letter, has agreed to a delay, but cautions the farmer that "gentlemen live at great expence" and "are obliged to keep up their part." The tenant thankfully promises great industry and grateful prayers "for his honour's health and prosperity" from his whole family, although three of his six children "can but lisp their prayers" (135).

Goodwill and trust in one another's integrity is shown to be the best course in the affairs of businessmen. A country trader, just setting up for himself, writes to a city dealer that as an apprentice he observed "the satisfaction you always gave my master in your dealings" and therefore he makes "an offer of my correspondence," noting that this cannot disoblige his former master "because of the distance I shall be from him" (35). The dealer accepts him as a client and promises that he will deal with him "on the same foot" as his former master, "not doubting you will make as punctual returns as he does; which entitles him to a more favourable usage than could otherwise be afforded." Letters 42 and 43 record a friendly exchange between a city dealer and a country trader over a debt, in which the debtor promises prompt payment and a resolution to be more punctual in the future, but letter 44 suggests that a harsher tone was sometimes necessary. It begins, "I am sorry that your ill usage constrains me to write to you in the most pressing manner," continuing, "Can you think it is possible to carry on business after the manner you act by me?" (49). He writes that this conduct "is a very bad compliment to my *prudence*" as well as to "your own *gratitude*," since "surely good usage should be intitled to good usage." While he "shall be very loth to take any harsh methods," he declares that "Trade is so dependent a thing . . . that it cannot be carried on without mutual punctuality." This letter also produces prompt results and a promise of amendment. In letter 60 a father cautions a son that "Remissness is inexcusable in all men, but in none so much as a man of business, the soul of which is industry, diligence and punctuality," and pictures "the indignities he is likely to suffer" (70) if he continues his idle habits. The son thanks him for his timely advice, promises reform, and notes that he has, in fact, already suffered "the insults of a creditor" (71).

This blend of strict standards with tolerance and understanding also characterizes the ideal suggested by Richardson's letters about family relations. Letter 56, from a father to an ungracious son, is typical of this group. The tone is reasonable and quiet, not harsh or threatening, and the father stresses the self-interest of the son as much as his own paternal rights or feelings. He is writing after many "solemn promises of amendment" have been broken, hoping that a letter may have more effect than "mere words" since it can be read and reread and may, perhaps, "give you *reflection,* and, by God's grace, bring on your *repentance* and *amendment*" (65). He asks first that his son "make *my* case *your own*; and think, if *you* were to be a Father of such a son, how his actions would grieve and afflict you," and then to consider the damage he is doing to his own health and to his reputation. He will end up able to associate only with the dregs of society and will be "miserable in *this world,* when you might be happy." Added to this prospect is the dread of what may be his lot in "*another world* beyond this transitory one." The father stresses the disinterestedness of himself and his wife, declaring, "we don't want anything of *you,* but *your own good,*" adding,

"Be but good to *yourself,* that is all we require of you" (66). He reminds his son that he is gifted with talents, pleads that he now demonstrate that his nature is "generous" rather than "sordid," and concludes by stressing "that no satisfaction, which is not grounded on virtue and sobriety, can be durable, or worthy of a rational creature." The letter is effective; the son resolves "instantly to set about a reformation," to "break myself from . . . frothy companions," and to seek his father's "direction for my future conduct" (68). A similar tone informs letter 36, in which a father tries to dissuade his son from "the Vice of drinking to Excess" (41). The chief argument is that the course of virtue is also the course of self-interest and the only one that will result in worldly happiness as well as salvation. Similar letters caution against forming unsuitable friendships and against extravagance, and use subtle flattery—"you do not want sense"—as well as reason.

While the age, in general, tended to grant absolute authority over children to parents, and especially to the father, Richardson's letters suggest mutual understanding and cooperation as preferable. Parents should understand their children, and also consult their wishes. The first letter in the collection gives friendly advice to a father who is planning to train his son to be a lawyer. The writer discourages this plan, noting his "good opinion of Will" who is "a modest, grave, sober youth" but doubting that he has "talents for the law, nor ever will have the presence of mind necessary to make a figure at the bar" (1). He also discourages a future as a physician, and urges a career that will "require no greater talents than he is possessed of," but one that will suit "the boy's turn of mind and inclination; which, I think, should always be consulted on these occasions" (4). The writer cautions against false snobbery and reminds the father "that most of the noble families in the kingdom, as well as the genteel ones, had the foundations of their grandeur laid in trade" (3).

By far the greatest number of letters in the collection are devoted to advice on courtship. This was the occasion perhaps most likely to produce conflict between parents and children. The moderate view in Richardson's age on relative rights of parents and children in deciding the choice of a spouse forbade children to marry without parents' consent but also gave children the right to veto a choice made by parents. Richardson's letters subscribe to this view, stressing that a wise and loving parent is always guided by a wish for the happiness of his child, not by sordid motives, and uses the greater wisdom of years and experience to steady the impulsive ardor of youth for the child's own

good. Certain kinds of suitors are to be disparaged automatically. In
letter 70 a father cautions his daughter against a "French Lover," writing, "His frothy behavior may divert well enough as an acquaintance;
but is very unsuitable, I think, to the character of a husband" (89). In
a similar vein, letter 9, in this case from an elder brother to a younger,
cautions against his infatuation with a "Lady of great Gaiety." "Her
airy flights, and gay behaviour are pleasing as a partner in conversation," he concedes, adding, "but will they be equally agreeable in a
partner for life?" (17). Perhaps one of the harshest letters in the collection is from a father to a daughter who encourages the addresses of a
subaltern. "Think well of the certain misery that must attend your
making such a choice," he writes, and asks, "If he be wise and indus-
trious how came he to prefer a life so mean and contemptible?" (77).
Another father refuses his consent to a match not only because he objects to the suitor, but because he considers his daughter too young.
"For consider," he writes, "you are not fully sixteen years of age; And
a wife, believe me, ought to have some better qualifications, than an
agreeable person, to *preserve an husband's esteem,* tho' it often is enough
to *attract a lover's notice*" (89).

Letter 66 is a letter from a daughter to her father pleading for a
sister who has married without his consent. She reports that her sister
is sorry for her fault, but she hopes that her husband's careful and
loving conduct to her will atone for his past wildness and that she will
be forgiven. The sister also points out that the match "now cannot be
helped" and that she hopes her father will "rather encourage [the young
man's] present resolutions by your kind favour, than make him despair
of a reconciliation, and so perhaps treat her with a negligence, which
hitherto she is not apprehensive of: For he is really very fond of her"
(84–85). The father replies that what she has done "is not *vicious* but
indiscreet," and that he still hopes for her happiness. He explains that
her husband has already come to ask for her fortune and that he made
it clear that "all she had to hope for was wholly at my disposal." He
tells the young man that he will "disburse it in such a manner as I
thought would most contribute to her advantage; and that as he was a
stranger to me, I should choose to know he *deserved* it, before he had
power over what I intended to do for her" (86). He notes, somewhat
cynically, "If he married her for *her own sake,* she will find no alteration
of behaviour from this disappointment: But if he married her only for
her *money,* she will soon be glad to find it in my possession rather
than his."

The proper protocol in courtship prescribed that the young man obtain the consent of the young lady's father before making a formal proposal of marriage. Richardson subscribed to this, and letters 15 through 21 follow the progress of an exemplary courtship. In the first letter, the daughter, who is living with her cousin at the time, tells her father of a proposal from an apparently eligible young man that has been made to her cousin, who has a high opinion of him. She, quite properly, has told the young man that she has "no thoughts of changing my condition . . . and should never think of it but in obedience to my parents" (25). The next two letters offer alternative responses, one a refusal based upon bad reports of the suitor's character, the other advising caution while the father can make inquiries. The daughter is instructed, "In the mean time, he may be told, that you are not at your own disposal, but entirely resolved to abide by my determination and direction, in an affair of this great importance: And this will put him upon applying to me, who, you need not doubt, will in this case, as in all others, study your good" (27). In letter 8 the suitor writes to the young lady's father, telling him of the "great value and affection I have for your worthy daughter" and assuring him that "I should think myself entirely unworthy of *her* favour, and of *your* approbation, if I could have a thought of influencing her resolution but in obedience to your pleasure" (28). He gives details of his financial position, his descent, and his character. The young lady's cousin affirms the truth of his statements in the next letter, urging the match, and in letter 15 the father replies to the suitor that his procedure in applying to him does "carry a very honourable appearance," but that his daughter is still very young to marry, adding, "I would not, for the world, in a case so nearly concerning her, and her future welfare, constrain her in the least" (30). The daughter is now to return home where her parents can "consult her inclinations," and the father affirms that he "shall then determine myself by that, and by what shall appear to offer most for her good." The suitor, after asking permission, writes to his beloved, "How happy should I be, if I could find my humble suit not quite indifferent to your dear self, and not rejected by him!" (31). He hopes that he will be given permission to visit them. An editorial insertion then explains that "the next steps to be taken being the inquiry into the truth of the young man's assertions, and a confirmation of his character; and then the proposals on the father's part of what he will give with his daughter," and since these are "done best by word of mouth, or interposition of friends; so shall we have no occasion to pursue this instance of courtship further" (32). The reader can only hope that this model pair were rewarded with a happy marriage.

The forms of courtship were seen as not merely tedious protocol, but as a protection, especially for young women, against future misery in an unsuitable match and against fortune hunters. Letter 53 warns a "young lady" against encouraging any clandestine address, arguing that a man who is worthy will never be afraid to appear openly; since no man can be ashamed of being known to love her, and that, "If he had not a meaner opinion of your understanding than he ought, he would not hope for success from such *poor methods*" (60). In another place, the advice is given that "if a young man has proposals to make, which he himself thinks would be accepted by a person of *years* and *experience,* he will apply in a regular way" (124). The prudent suitor, however, tries to ingratiate himself with the young woman as well as with her father. Letter 13 applies to a father for leave to address his daughter, but the young man is careful also to address himself to his beloved, informing her of an intended visit and declaring that he is her "most devoted humble Servant" (24).

Less formality was expected in lower class courtships. Letter 28 is from a maid servant in town to her parents telling them of an offer of marriage from a glazier. "He is a young man of sober character," she writes, adding, "has a good business . . . and is well beloved and spoken of by every one" (37), assuring them that her master and mistress approve. Her parents reply that "distance from you must make us leave everything to your own discretion," and that since she, as well as her master and mistress, are so well satisfied with his character, "we give our blessings and consents with all our hearts," only regretting that "we can do no more for you," but promising "some little matters, as far as we are able, towards house-keeping." The next letter informs them of her marriage and assures them that she "told him the naked truth of everything," so that they should not "straighten yourselves out of love to me," adding that her new husband "joins me in saying so" and "fears not to maintain me very well." She declares, "I have no reason to doubt of being very happy" (38).

Other courtship sequences explore variations on these models, including letters in which the lady declines the advances of a hopeful suitor, and another in which the young man, seeing no hope of success, withdraws his suit. Letter 89 ridicules "romantic rhapsody" in a letter in which the suitor treats his mistress as a goddess, while in letter 85 a gentleman resents the unworthy airs of coquetry that his beloved assumes. In letter 91 a father writes to his daughter of three suitors for her whom he has rejected—one is stupid, one is a libertine, and the other is a sot who promises reform—then continues to recommend an older man of character and position. He is careful to note that his choice "has good *health,* good *spirits,* and good *humour*; and is not yet got quite at the top of the *hill of life*" (116). The daughter rejects this suggestion, noting that "likeness of years [is] attended with likeness of humours" and that this is "a defect that will be far from mending by time" (117). Her father replies that he will never compel her inclinations, but continues to urge the match, noting that the difference in age is only ten years and asking that she permit Mr. Rowe to call on her two or three times to see if his conversation will incline her in his favor.

Courtships by both widows and widowers are discouraged, especially if either has children and more especially if the new spouse is younger. Indeed, financial necessity on the part of a widow seems the only justification for her remarriage. Richardson's position on this question was consonant with his time; most writers found the seekers after new young spouses figures of fun, especially widows, and the wicked stepmother is a cliché in fiction of the time. Richardson himself did, of course, remarry, but not until after the death of his children by his first marriage.

The letters that give advice on marriage also generally follow·the prevailing spirit of the times in urging the wife to be conciliatory in order to produce a happy marriage. Letter 146 is from a mother to a "high-spirited" daughter, declaring "Prudence will oblige a good wife to bear a little contradiction from her husband, tho' not always just, perhaps, as well as to avoid giving offence" (183). She continues, "Suppose he is peevish, petulant, uneasy in his temper, . . . must *you* be peevish and petulant because *he* is so?," and advises, "If you love him as you ought, you will extenuate his failings" (184). She tells her daughter that, while the combination of a henpecked husband and a termagant wife are objects of ridicule, "meekness, condescension and forbearance . . . are the *glory* of [our sex]," and she reminds her daughter that she "has vow'd obedience and duty" (185). She counsels, "First soften him by good temper; then, when soften'd, expostulate mildly on the unreasonableness of his anger," hoping that he will "see you advise him for his good" (186). In letter 54, a mother writes to a daughter who is jealous of her husband. She first covers all possibilities by noting, "You either *have,* or *have not,* cause for it" (61). In the first case, the wife should examine her own conduct to see if she by any "disagreeableness of behaviour" has alienated her husband's affections "and if so, set about amending, in order to recover them." If this fails, at least she will "have nothing to reproach *yourself* with." The mother explains that "the creatures wicked men follow omit nothing to oblige them," and therefore she must show her husband "that such creatures shall not outdo you in an *obliging behaviour,* and *sweetness of temper,*" hoping that "in *time*" he "will be softened by your softness. But, the mother warns, "if you make his home uneasy to him, he will fly both *that* and *you.*" If her jealousy is based not upon proven fact, but merely on gossip, she is, of course, even more at fault. "Softness and kind expostulation" are the only ways to hope for happiness, and, at the worst, she can gain "comfort and patience in *your own* innocence," confident she will gain reward after "this transitory life" (64). The ideal of a mutually happy marriage is shown in letter 128 and 129, an exchange between a husband serving in the navy and his wife at home.

Some isolated letters seem to give Richardson an opportunity to air personal opinions, such as shock at the conduct exhibited at public executions (letter 160), ridicule of fashionable fads (125), the uselessness of going to law (144), the callousness of those who find Bedlam (the hospital for the insane) amusing (163), disapproval of manly airs in young women and of the new style in riding habits that with "a cock'd hat, a lac'd jacket, a fop's peruke," creates "such a *boy-girl* figure" that could be becoming only to a "young Italian singer" (114) (letter 90). Still other letters give the reader of the novels, now gifted with hindsight, glimpses into Richardson's future fictions. Letter 138, from a father to a daughter urging her to leave a master who has made an attempt on her virtue, prefigures *Pamela,* while letter 133, from a lady to an unwelcome suitor who has the approval of her parents, echoes the arguments Clarissa will use with Solmes. "If I have the misfortune to know I cannot love you," the young lady writes, "will not *justice* to yourself, if not *pity* to me, oblige you to abandon your present purpose?" (159). She asks him, "Why should you make a poor creature unhappy in the displeasure of all her friends at present, and still more unhappy, if, to avoid that, she gives up her *person* where she cannot bestow her *heart*? If you love me, as you profess, is it for *my* sake or is it for *your own*?," adding, "Who, that *truly* loves, wishes to make the object of his love miserable?" (160). Letters 161 to 165, a correspondence between an aunt and her niece about two suitors, shows us, in the niece, a foretaste of the satirical vein often adopted by Anna

Howe and Charlotte Grandison. One suitor is an egotistical fop who is
justly derided, while the other is a worthy man but perhaps too grave
and serious. The style here, as the niece gives "an instance of Mr.
Rushford's *grave airs*," prefigures Richardson the novelist. After an
afternoon spat, caused chiefly by the niece's purposeful misunderstanding of her serious suitor, Mr. Rushford comes in the evening, hoping
to make up the quarrel. "*I see you are angry with me, madam.*—I am
sorry for it sir, said I. *Sorry for your anger, I hope, madam.*—I should be
sorry, sir, said I, if any body should see me angry for nothing." The
verbal fencing continues until the poor suitor declares, "What's sport
to you, is death to me" (224). The use of brief interchanges of dialogue,
often without interruption of quotation marks, is characteristic of
scenes in *Sir Charles Grandison* where Harriet Byron similarly describes
suitors she finds amusing or Charlotte Grandison describes her contests
with Lord G., her future husband. Like Charlotte, the niece obviously
enjoys the perquisites granted to the woman in courtship and cannot
resist teasing. Her aunt warns her, "the more obliging you are in the
time of *your power,* the more it will move a generous mind to indulge
you, in *his*; and the time you may reckon yours, may not be three
months in proportion to thirty years of his" (229). Charlotte is similarly chided by Harriet and by her brother for her imperious behaviour.
    Richardson interrupted his work on the *Familiar Letters* to write
Pamela, thus beginning his career as a novelist. *Pamela* was followed
by a sequel and then by *Clarissa* and *Sir Charles Grandison.* Fame
brought Richardson new friends, such as Lady Bradshaigh, but
changed his life very little. He remained the somewhat shy and private
person he had always been, occupied with his business, enjoying the
company of friends in his family circle, and writing letters. He revised
the novels many times, and published works connected with them:
Clarissa's supposed book of meditations, *Meditations Collected from the
Sacred Books,* and, for the buyers of the early editions, *Letters and Passages Restored from the Original Manuscripts of the History of Clarissa,* as
well as *A Collection of the Moral and Instructive Sentiments, Maxims, Cautions, and Reflections, Contained in the Histories of Pamela, Clarissa, and
Sir Charles Grandison.* In response to the pirating of Sir Charles Grandison by the Irish publisher George Faulkner, Richardson published
pamphlets, *An Address to the Public,* and *The Case of Samuel Richardson,*
explaining his position. He refused the pleas of readers for a continuation of *Sir Charles.* His later writings also might be said to include
his advice to Edward Young on *Conjectures on Original Composition,* ad-

vice so extensive and substantive that the published work is virtually a collaboration.[34] After the publication of *Pamela,* Richardson systematically saved copies of his letters, which are interesting both for the light they give on his character and opinions and as informal literary criticism of his own works.

Richardson lived to be seventy-one, dying of a stroke. During his last years he permitted himself some relaxation from his former regime—rising at five in the morning and retiring to rest at eleven—now allowing himself to be "sometimes indulged in bed till seven."[35] He attained the allotted three score and ten, continuing his customary quiet course of life—that of the prudent business man, the constant friend, the good husband, the loving father—and, most importantly for us, having demonstrated himself a great artist.

Chapter Two
Pamela and Its Sequel

Pamela, Richardson's first novel, was an instant success. Not only was it a best-seller, going into five editions in its first year, but it gained the approbation of both the pious and the discerning. Dr. Slocock, a well-known London preacher, recommended it from the pulpit, and Alexander Pope praised it. It became so much the rage in fashionable circles that ladies carried fans adorned with scenes from the work. This acceptance was important not merely as a passing fad, but as an indication of the new status it conferred on a formerly scorned genre—the novel. Before Richardson, prose fiction held approximately the same standing in the literary hierarchy as adventure comic books or formula romances do today. Novels were automatically disparaged as worthless, if not actually harmful. They were usually written by hacks to eke out a precarious living and designed for an audience that enjoyed vicarious thrills, improbable plots, and thinly disguised sexual titillation.[1] No respectable adult admitted to reading them, let alone writing them. The frontispiece of Pope's *Dunciad* shows an ass with panniers well laden primarily with such works of fiction.

Richardson was, of course, well aware of this, and his own works are in a certain sense antinovels. He described the impulse that led to the writing of *Pamela* in a letter to his friend, Aaron Hill. While he was working on the *Familiar Letters* he remembered a story that had been told to him many years before about a beautiful young serving girl who resisted her master's attempts to seduce her until, finally, won over by her virtue, he married her. "Little did I think," Richardson writes, " of making one, much less two volumes of it. But," he continues, "when I began to recollect what had, so many years before, been told me by my friend, I thought the story, if written in an easy and natural manner, suitably to the simplicity of it, might possibly introduce a new species of writing."[2] Richardson was quite aware that he was an innovator, introducing "a new species of writing." His letter then states that this new species "might possibly turn young people into a course of reading different from the pomp and parade of romance-writing, and dismissing the improbable and marvellous, with which novels generally abound, might tend to promote the cause of religion and virtue."

Moral instruction, then, was Richardson's declared purpose in writing. This attitude was not unusual in his time. Richardson's contemporaries would have acceded to such an aim, and even fiction that described the far from virtuous careers of rascals or ladies of pleasure justified itself by ending with a cautionary moral. Johnson, in *Rambler* no. 4, spoke for his age in asserting that novels "serve as lectures of conduct and introductions into life" and that therefore they should exhibit "the most perfect idea of virtue."[3] As we have seen, Richardson used the format of a book of model letters as an opportunity to write a work that was in fact a disguised conduct book; this didactic motive informs his works of fiction as well. The moral tone of *Pamela,* then, accounts for its acceptance by the pious, but does not account either for its enormous popular appeal or for its aesthetic success. It is to the first part of Richardson's statement, his use of "an easy and natural manner", that we must turn to explain why *Pamela* was indeed "a new species of writing."

The plot of *Pamela* is a simple one and follows very closely the anecdote that Richardson recounted in his letter to Hill. Pamela is a beautiful young girl of fifteen whose parents have come down in their fortunes through no fault of their own. She has gone into service, and her mistress, recognizing her abilities and charmed by her goodness, has made a special pet of her, instructing her in writing, in casting accounts, and even in playing the spinet, so that she is, as she herself puts it, "qualified above my degree."[4] As the book opens, Pamela's mistress has just died, and her son, Mr. B., is now master of the household. Pamela fears that she will be dismissed, since she is no longer needed in her post as waiting maid, but her new employer reassures her that he will keep her on to care for his fine linen. Pamela is happy that she will not become a burden on her already straitened parents, but they immediately suspect Mr. B.'s motives, warning her to be careful. It is soon clear that he is indeed attracted to the pretty maid, and Pamela, fearing further advances, asks to return home. Mrs. Jervis, the kindly housekeeper, persuades her to stay long enough to finish a waistcoat she is embroidering for the master, but finally she is permitted to leave for her parents' house in Mr. B.'s coach. She is not taken home, however, but abducted and carried to Mr. B.'s Lincolnshire estate where she is kept a prisoner by the wicked housekeeper, Mrs.

Jewkes. All her endeavors to gain help are fruitless, except for the sympathy of an ineffectual curate, Mr. Williams, and her efforts to escape fail. Despairing, she even contemplates suicide. Finally, Mr. B. arrives, trying to persuade her to become his mistress on generous terms and threatening force if she refuses. However, when he obtains the letter-journal that Pamela has been secretly writing, he is touched by her distress and convinced of her innocence. Mr. B. now realizes that the only way he can have Pamela, whom he loves more than ever, is by marriage, and after a struggle with his pride he proposes. Some misunderstandings ensue, but at last the pair are married. The final third of the book shows us Pamela in her new role, winning the admiration of high and low alike.

Certainly, this summary of the plot does not seem to account for the extraordinary appeal of *Pamela*. Why did this rather trite Cinderella story have such marked success in capturing its readers? The answer lies in Richardson's narrative method. The novel is told in letters, almost all of which are written by Pamela, so that the reader learns of events directly from her without the intervention of a narrator. This use of an epistolary style undoubtedly had advantages for the diffident Richardson, who was acutely conscious of the fact that he lacked the classical education and intellectual background considered necessary for an author, because the device of writing in letters allows the narrative to be composed by Pamela, a young girl with only "common school learning" herself. She speaks in her own voice, and Richardson's use of colloquial diction, criticized by some contemporaries, adds liveliness and verisimilitude to her account. Even more important for the reader, however, was Richardson's technique of "writing to the moment," as he termed his "new Manner of Writing."[5] He explained that his aim was to convey "those lively and delicate Impressions, which *Things Present* are known to make upon the Minds of those affected by them," asserting that "in the Study of human Nature the Knowledge of those Apprehensions leads us farther into the Recesses of the human Mind, than the colder and more general Reflections suited to a continued . . . Narrative."[6]

Richardson believed that moral lessons could best be conveyed by presenting exemplary characters. The writer should give readers a standard of behavior to emulate, rather than only condemning evil through the depiction of wicked characters. A negative example, Richardson thought, might encourage a smug reaction whereby the reader can contentedly feel superior despite his own faults, and therefore "a faulty or vicious Character will be considered rather as an acquittal than a Condemnation."[7] Lovelace, the villain of *Clarissa,* takes pleasure, for example, in pointing out that King David was guilty of crimes. However, exemplary characters, in order to be effective, must gain the emotional sympathy of the reader. The more closely readers identified with his characters, Richardson believed, the more telling the moral lesson would become. By "writing to the moment" he enabled readers to follow the inward struggles of Pamela, to participate in her uncertainties, and to undergo her trials. The psychological vividness he achieved by this method was responsible for the unparalleled effectiveness of *Pamela.* The villagers of Slough, we are told, who gathered to hear *Pamela* read aloud, rang the church bells in celebration when they reached the account of her marriage. Richardson's method also captured more sophisticated readers. Lady Mary Wortley Montagu wrote to her daughter, "This Richardson is a strange Fellow. I heartily despise him and eagerly read him, nay sob over his works in a most scandalous manner."[8]

Through Pamela's letters and journal, then, the reader shares her uncertainties and fears, living entirely in the present. This method, as Richardson later explained, gives "opportunities to describe the agitations that fill the heart, in the progress of a material and interesting subject, the event of which remains undecided."[9] While the form of a retrospective first-person narrative, a fictional autobiography, does give opportunities to reveal the thoughts and inner turmoil of the protagonist, it also gives an important cue to the reader—the narrator has survived the depicted trials, emerging with sufficient physical and psychological strength to write the story. The narrator is also at a distance from the events that are described, recalling the past, usually from a position of relative tranquillity. Richardson's method plunges his readers into greater uncertainties, forcing us to participate fully in Pamela's fluctuating fortunes.

The novel opens with the words "I have great trouble," setting the mood of emotional tension and the sense of immediacy so characteristic of the work. The letters are sometimes broken off at a moment of suspense, as in letter 15 when she tells of a forthcoming interview with Mr. B., writing, "O how I dread this to-morrow's appearance! . . . O this frightful to-morrow! how I dread it!" The letter is unsigned, and the next letter takes up the story. "Well, you may believe how uneasily I passed the time till his appointed hour came . . . and sometimes I had great courage, and sometimes none at all," she records, telling of her attempts to inspirit herself—" 'O Pamela,' said I to myself, 'why art thou so foolish and fearful? Thou hast done no harm!' "—and of her fluctuating feelings—"So I cheered myself, but yet my poor heart sunk . . . I dreaded [the moment], and yet I wished it to come" (21). In other instances the letters are broken off because of events in the narrative. Letter 14, for example, ends hastily, and Pamela begins the next by explaining "I broke off abruptly my last letter; for I feared he was coming; and so it happened" (18). Letter 23 is interrupted when Pamela is called to present herself to satisfy the curiosity of some neighboring ladies. "I believe they are coming," she writes, "and I will tell you the rest by-and-by. I wish they had come and were gone. . . . Well, these fine ladies have been here, and are gone back again" (38–39). Later, when Pamela is confined in Lincolnshire, she is again told to prepare for a visit from some curious ladies. As she waits, she impatiently writes, "And no young ladies!—So that I fancy—But hold! I hear them in the coach, I believe. I'll step to the window" (158). The letter continues, "What will become of me? Here is my master come in his fine chariot! Indeed he is! What shall I do?" Two hours later, she records "Though I dread to see him, yet I wonder I have not," and notes her poor penmanship, "How crooked and trembling the lines!— I must leave off till I can get quieter fingers!" (159). We are left in suspense until the next morning when Pamela recounts that later "I heard his voice on the stairs, as he was coming up to me." Richardson here incorporates the homely detail that makes the novel so vivid—"It was about his supper; for he said, 'I shall choose a boiled chicken with butter and parsley.' And up he came" (159).

In *Pamela* the reader experiences the events of the novel entirely through the consciousness of the heroine herself. This accounts for the chief strengths of the work—the delineation of Pamela's inner struggles and the concomitant identification of the reader with these struggles—but it also leads to problems. From the outset, in the midst of the general acclaim for *Pamela* there were negative voices. These critics saw Richardson's heroine as a designing hypocrite who tempts the naive Mr. B. and follows the path of virtue only to gain worldly fortune. Fielding's *Shamela* is the most telling of the anti-Pamelas. He parodies Richardson's style, exaggerating the use of "low" language—"No, forsooth, says I, as pertly as I could; why how now saucy chops, boldface, says he—"[10] and of detail—"my little all . . . being no more than two day-caps, two night-caps, five shifts, one sham, a hoop, a quilted petticoat, two flannel-petticoats, two pair of stockings, one odd one, a pair of lac'd shoes, a short flowered apron, a lac'd neck-handkerchief, one clog, and almost another, and some few books . . ." (327)—as well as the method of writing in the present—"Odsbobs! I hear him just coming in at the door. You see I write in the present tense . . ." (313)—but, more importantly, calls into question the moral basis of the work. Fielding christens Mr. B. Mr. Booby and has Shamela declare, "I thought once of making a little fortune by my person. I now intend to make a great one by my vartue" (325). Critics of *Pamela,* both in its own time and today, have focused on three major questions: what is the motive behind Pamela's resistance—is it only prudential or is it based upon greater values?; does Pamela's acceptance of Mr. B. as a husband negate her previous struggles—is he a lecherous cad unworthy of her love or are his actions in part excusable in the context of his society?; and, finally, what does "virtue" mean in the novel—does it connote only physical chastity or does it embrace a fuller range of qualities? Richardson was aware that his method of "writing to the moment" demanded attentive readers: "the world is not enough used to this way of writing," he noted, explaining that mistakes resulted from not regarding the fact that "in the minutiae lie often the unfoldings of the Story, as well as of the heart."[11] In *Pamela* these difficulties are increased by Richardson's use of a single point of view.

What is the basis of Pamela's resistance? It is, of course, her own moral code, which can accept sexual pleasure only when sanctified by marriage. Pamela is the child of two good, pious, uncompromising Christians. The only letters in the novel not written by Pamela herself are written by her father, and we learn at firsthand of her parents' strict morality. Although very poor, they are hesitant to accept her gift of four guineas because it has come from the hand of Mr. B., whom they suspect of ulterior motives. Only when she assures them that the sum was found in the pocket of her dead mistress and that it is customary for a waiting maid to be given such coins, do they feel comfortable about receiving them. Pamela has been well taught by them and shares their unswerving adherence to both the spirit and the letter of the laws of traditional moral conduct. Furthermore, her determination is reinforced by a sense of her own worth. She insists that she must be treated as an individual in her own right, not simply as a means of gratification for another. Pamela is not a social revolutionary; she acknowledges the great distance between herself and Mr. B. Indeed, she naively reassures her parents that their early fears must be groundless, writing, "for I am sure my master would not demean himself so as to think upon such a poor girl as I for my harm" (7). After his first advances, an attempt to kiss her in the garden summer house, Mr. B. declares, "What a foolish hussey you are!" and asks, "have I done you any harm?" Pamela replies, "Yes Sir, the greatest harm in the world: you have taught me to forget myself, and what belongs to me, and have lessened the distance that fortune has made between us, by demeaning yourself, to be so free to a poor servant" (12). And even after Mr. B. has virtually proposed to her, when he asks her advice about marrying her she tells him, "I must needs say, that I think you ought to regard the world's opinion" (189). However, even the lowly have rights, primarily the right to their own personal integrity, and Pamela, in the midst of her trials declares, "My *soul* is of equal importance with the soul of a princess, though my quality is inferior to that of the meanest slave" (137).

The conflict between Pamela and Mr. B. is really the opposition of two systems of values. In seeking her for his mistress Mr. B. is trying to make Pamela accede to the code which is permissible in his world, but she insists upon maintaining her own moral standards. Use of language emphasizes this contrast. Pamela comments that, if she had yielded to Mr. B. then, "my *crime* would have been my *virtue* with him" (17), and, after his promises to maintain her she notes, " 'Tis true, he promises honour, and all that; but the honour of the wicked is disgrace and shame to the virtuous" (106). When Mrs. Jewkes scoffs at her fears, saying "Your *ruin*!—Why ne'er a lady in the land may live happier than you, if you will, or be more honourably used," Pamela refuses to debate, explaining, "Well, Mrs. Jewkes, I shall not at this time dispute with you about the words *ruin* and *honourable*; for I find we have quite different notions of both" (118).

Pamela's pride helps to support her in this conflict. In creating exemplary characters Richardson did not intend to create perfect characters. He believed that in order to promote sympathetic identification by readers, which he saw as the chief means of moral instruction, his characters must be credible, not coldly ideal. He wrote that "The character of a mere Mortal cannot, ought not, to be quite perfect,"[12] and declared to a friend, "I have generally taken Human Nature *as it is*; for it is to no purpose to suppose it Angelic, or to endeavour to make it so."[13] Pamela does, indeed, have failings, and pride is the most notable. She confides to her parents in one of her early letters that "there is a secret pleasure one has to hear one's self praised" (5), and during her captivity, in the midst of plans to escape, she writes, "O the pride, thought I, I shall have, if I can secure my innocence, and escape the artful wiles of this wicked master!" (96). Pamela's considerable share of egotism is in one sense a defect, and her lack of self-knowledge can lead to comedy, but it can also be seen as both justified and sustaining. An important scene early in the novel illustrates this. Pamela has been told that her request will be granted, and that she is to be sent back to live with her parents. Realizing that the fine clothes that her mistress has given her will be unsuitable in humble rustic surroundings, Pamela has made herself a new country costume. She writes of going up to her room where "I dressed myself in my new garb," giving details of gown, cap, shoes, and stockings, and "When I was quite equipped, I took my straw hat in my hand, with its two blue strings, and looked in the glass, as proud as any thing. To say truth, I never liked myself so well in my life" (42). Pamela then adds, "O the pleasure of descending with ease, innocence, and resignation!—Indeed, there is nothing like it! An humble mind, I plainly see, cannot meet with any shocking disappointment, let Fortune's wheel turn round as it will." On one plane Pamela's self-satisfaction as she congratulates herself on her humility is simply amusing. In reading the passage it is important to be aware that we must separate Richardson the author from his creation. While Pamela may not perceive the comedy intrinsic in praising oneself for "an humble mind," Richardson certainly did. On another level, however, Pamela's self-praise is correct. She has resisted the temptation of gaining material luxuries by forfeiting her own code of values and, far from feeling downcast, she looks forward with undaunted spirits to assuming her new role, although she is quite aware of the discomforts the change will bring about—"It may be a little hard at first," she writes her parents, and tells of trying to scour a pewter plate, declaring, "I could do it by degrees; it only blistered my hands in two places" (63). Pamela is not going to emphasize her sacrifice by dressing drably—the cap has a green knot, the blue worsted stockings have white clocks, the homespun gown is faced with pretty printed calico, and the plain shoes are still "what they call Spanish leather." She can rightfully be pleased with herself, therefore, not only because she looks fetching, but because her new clothes represent a spiritual victory and emphasize her lack of self-pity in the face of changing fortune. The episode also shows us, however, that Pamela is a very believable young girl who is proud of her good looks and even of her cleverness, telling her parents, "You'll say I was no bad house-wife" (33). We can correctly accuse Pamela of being vain, but we also recognize the important role that her sense of her own value plays in her struggle.

Pride can be spiritually dangerous, however, as Pamela learns. She has determined to make a final attempt to escape after hearing that her only ally, Mr. Williams, has been jailed and that Mr. B. is soon coming to Lincolnshire. She plans to squeeze through the bars on the chamber window, drop down to the projecting roof of the parlor, then to the ground, and, leaving a petticoat and neckerchief floating in the pond as a false scent, use a key she has procured to open the garden gate to freedom. Her scheme proves abortive because Mrs. Jewkes has changed the padlock. Pamela then tries to climb the wall, but she falls, injuring herself, when the bricks give way under her hand. She limps back to the pond, thinks of the evils which confront her, and contemplates suicide, indulging in the common childhood fantasy that all will "then be moved to lament their misdoings . . . when they see the dead corpse of the unhappy Pamela" (150). She soon realizes that she is succumbing to the sin of despair. Writing to her parents she rejoices that she managed to overcome "an enemy she never thought of before . . . the weakness and presumption of her own mind" (148), meditating that perhaps her sufferings are designed by God "to make me rely solely on his grace and assistance, who, perhaps, have too much prided myself in a vain dependence on my own foolish contrivances."

The reader who attends to the "minutiae" does get a valid portrait of Pamela which, faults and all, is a convincing picture of a lively, honest, virtuous, and innocent young woman, a young woman whose behavior is grounded both in firm moral beliefs and in her assertion of her right to preserve her personal integrity and to maintain her own standards of value. Richardson's one-sided narrative makes it more difficult, however, to get a well-balanced view of Mr. B., whom we see solely through Pamela's eyes. The only letters by Mr. B. in the narrative are those related to us by Pamela. They have been written very deliberately to achieve an end, and are the opposite of the artless spontaneity that Richardson felt reveals "the agitations which fill the heart." We never learn at firsthand of Mr. B's doubts, hesitations, or inner struggles, as we do of Pamela's. The reader must therefore read even more carefully to get a true picture of him, and this is indeed a flaw in the novel, a flaw that Richardson was to correct in the more complex design of *Clarissa*.

Is Mr. B.'s conduct so reprehensible that he forfeits all claim to be a suitable husband for Pamela? The twentieth-century reader must first make allowances for the prevailing mores of Mr. B.'s society. As we have seen, the difference between his values and Pamela's is pointed out by their contrasting use of such words as "virtue" and "honor." In the world of the aristocratic rake a woman, and especially a lower-class woman, is fair game as long as she is properly compensated afterward. When Sir Simon Darnford is asked to help Pamela, he says to his wife, "Why, what is all this, my dear, but that our neighbor has a mind to his mother's waiting-maid! And if he takes care she wants for nothing, I don't see any great injury will be done her. He hurts no *family* by this" (116). Even Mr. Peters, the minister of the parish, refuses to intervene, explaining that "it was too common and fashionable a case to be withstood by a private clergyman" (116), and, noting that Mr. B. "promises to do honourably by her," declares that "he is no covetous or wicked gentleman, except in this case; and 'tis what all young gentlemen will do" (117). None of the contemporary disparagers of *Pamela* suggested that the imprisonment was improbable—a telling indication of the power of wealth, but most of all the prevalence of a double standard of sexual morality. In *Spectator,* no. 2, for example, Addison introduces Will Honeycomb, a member of the club, explaining "where women are not concerned, he is an honest, worthy man."[14] In the novel the reader is certainly not asked to condone Mr. B.'s conduct, but an eighteenth-century audience would have understood that his actions were consonant with a largely accepted and tolerated code.

Because we see only through Pamela's eyes, Mr. B.'s conduct is apt to seem more threatening than it actually is. Pamela has been warned by her parents to be suspicious of him, and this warning is soon justified by his embraces in the summer house. Pamela describes the incident to her parents in highly colored language—"Now, you will say, all his wickedness appeared plainly. I struggled and trembled, and was so benumbed with terror, that I sunk down, not in a fit, and yet not myself; and I found myself in his arms, quite void of strength, and he kissing me two or three times with frightful eagerness" (12). Despite being "quite void of strength," she does manage to "burst from him," and he reassures her, "I'll do you no harm, Pamela; don't be afraid of me." Mr. B.'s conduct is certainly not exemplary, but the reader should understand, even if Pamela herself is quite naturally too upset to be objective, that what has actually happened is that Mr. B., attracted by Pamela's beauty, has ventured a few kisses to test her reaction. He would have every reason to expect that a naive young girl of fifteen, awed by his wealth and position, would be considerably more compliant than Pamela. Mr. B. later explains to Mrs. Jervis, the good housekeeper, "I think her very pretty, and I thought her humble . . .

but I abhor the thought of forcing her to anything," adding, "I was bewitched by her, I think, to be freer than became me" (23). Mr. B. has his own suspicions to contend with, chiefly the fear that Pamela is indeed, as the anti-Pamelas asserted, designing and hypocritical. Even after he has proposed to Pamela, he must be reassured that she loves him for himself alone, asking her "And were I not what I am, could you give me the *preference* to any other you know in the world?" (241). Now, when Mrs. Jervis defends her he responds, "O the little hypocrite, she has all the arts of her sex; they were *born* with her; I told you awhile ago you did not know her" (24). He agrees to let Pamela return to her family, observing that, "it is best for her and me too" and marveling "where she had it, I can't tell; but I never met with the fellow of her in my life" (26). Mr. B., aware of his own personal attractions and conditioned by the code of the gentleman rake, finds it hard to believe that Pamela's resistance is genuine. His incredulity does lead him to test her again and again, but the reader should also realize that Pamela's fears sometime exaggerate his actions. This is the problem inherent in Richardson's use of a single point of view. The more skillfully he manages to promote the reader's identification with Pamela, the harder it is for the reader to be objective, and the more likely it is that Pamela's perceptions will be accepted as truth.

Mr. B. is a bit of a bumbler, and he is an egotistical aristocratic male, but he is not a deep-dyed villain. He tells Pamela, "You know I am not a very abandoned profligate: I have hitherto been guilty of no very enormous or vile actions" (188). A careful assessment of his conduct leads the reader to agree. Despite ample opportunity, especially when Pamela is imprisoned in Lincolnshire with the wicked Mrs. Jewkes as warder, he does not rape Pamela. Mrs. Jewkes, in fact, is impatient with him, urging, "What you do, Sir, do: don't stand, dilly dallying," and assuring him, "she'll be quieter when she knows the worst" (179).

Mrs. Jervis, early in the novel, explains Mr. B.'s quandary to Pamela: "He has a noble estate; and yet I believe he loves you, though his servant, better than all the ladies in the land; he has tried to overcome it, because you are so much his inferior; and it is my opinion he finds he can't; and that vexes his proud heart" (29). This is an accurate summary, one that Mr. B. himself echoes just before he proposes to Pamela. He tells her, "I cannot live without you; and I would divide, with all my soul, my estate with you, to make you mine on my own terms. These you have absolutely rejected," he continues, and asks, "But what can I do? Consider the pride of my condition . . . how then, with the distance between us in the world's judgement, can I think of making you my wife?" (188). For Mr. B. the world's judgment includes that of his fellow libertines. He will have to withstand "the ridicule and rude jests of his equals, and companions" (304). His marriage to Pamela will be an open admission that he has yielded to her terms, that despite his advantages of position, wealth, and free access he has been unable to seduce her, an admission that leaves him open to the charge most damaging to the male ego—that of sexual inadequacy. Fielding's *Shamela* does, in fact, emphasize this.

Mr. B.'s conduct, then, while far from exemplary, can be somewhat excused when we understand the social and psychological pressures governing his actions. After his reform Pamela herself is more than willing to see him in the most favorable light because, from the beginning of the novel, she has been attracted to him. The reader is aware of this long before Pamela. In the first letter, she tells how she is surprised by Mr. B. while writing. She is "all in confusion" (2), although she remarks, "Yet I know not for what," adding a significant clue for us, "Indeed he is the best of gentlemen, I think." Pamela is conscious that the great social gap between them would seem to preclude marriage, and therefore she is reluctant to recognize that she is, in fact, in love with Mr. B. During her captivity, she writes, "What is the matter, that, with all his ill usage of me, I cannot hate him?," adding, "and oh what an angel would he be in my eyes yet, if he would cease his attempts and reform!" (156). Pamela's attraction to her persecutor is potentially her greatest weakness, as she recognizes, declaring, "I have withstood his *anger*; but may I not relent at his kindness? How shall I stand *that*?" (70). Pamela is truly exemplary because she resists not merely the material inducements Mr. B. offers but her own sexual desires. After Mr. B. has proposed to her, she is warned by an anonymous letter that he intends to trick her with a sham marriage ceremony. She is more vulnerable now to his plots because she has relaxed her guard. "I found, before, to my grief," she explains to her parents, "that my heart was too partial in his favor; but *now* . . . I am quite overcome" (220). She berates her "treacherous heart" that has been betrayed by kindness when it had "so well maintained thy post against the most violent and avowed, and therefore, as I thought, more dangerous attacks!" (221). Pamela confesses that she will "never be able to think of any body in the world but him" (222) and, when the letter is proved false, her acceptance of Mr. B. as a husband is not surprising.

Pamela's resistance, then, is not merely prudential, and it is not necessarily invalidated by her marriage. What, however, is the meaning of "virtue" in the novel? Is it, as Fielding implied, confined narrowly to physical chastity? Or does the novel suggest a more generous spectrum of values? Pamela herself, while quite naturally averse to being sexually violated, makes a clear moral distinction between an intact maidenhead and errant desire. She replies to Mr. B.'s threats that "if I cannot escape the violence of man, I hope, by God's grace, I shall have nothing to reproach myself, for not doing all in my power to avoid my disgrace," declaring that she will be guiltless because her "will bore no part in the violation" (167). Mr. B.'s hierarchy of values is also more complex than a hasty assessment of his conduct might suggest. While it is Pamela's beauty that first attracts Mr. B., even very early in the novel he makes it clear that other qualities are of greater value. When some neighbors knowingly joke about his finding merit in his mother's pretty maid, he declares, "I don't know how it is, but I see with different eyes from other people," and after acknowledging that she is indeed "well enough" he asserts that "her greatest excellence is, that she is humble and courteous, and faithful, and makes all her fellow-servants love her" (38). It is insight into her thoughts gained through reading her candid letters that finally determines him to marry her. On their marriage night he tells her, "I am the conquest more of your virtue than your beauty" (315). This "virtue" encompasses more than mere resistance; it is, in fact, Pamela's generosity of spirit that finally brings the two together.

After Pamela receives the anonymous warning that Mr. B. is planning a sham marriage, her cold behavior puzzles him and he warns her, "you must not give me cause to think you will be more insolent, as you find me kinder" (202). Her renewed request to be allowed to return to her parents enrages him, and he asks, "Is it *thus* in my fond conceding moments, that I am to be answered and despised?," advising Pamela to "know as well how to behave in a hopeful prospect, as in a distressful state" (214). He does then send her back to her parents, but he also continues to read the journal that he has forced her to give him. Finding that his love is further increased and that he cannot part with her, he sends after her, leaving her a free choice whether to return to him or to go to her family, but hoping that "if you are the generous Pamela I imagine you to be . . . you can forgive the man who loves you more than himself" (223). Pamela justifies his confidence even though she realizes that if he betrays her, she will now seem to have no excuse, "for the world, the *wise* world, that never is wrong itself, judges always by events. And if he should use me ill, then I shall be blamed for trusting him" (224). Pamela says of his conduct, "Now this is a dear generous manner of treating me. O how I love to be generously used!" (224). Mr. B. loves to be generously used also, and the pair are at last happily united.

The actual marriage ceremony takes place approximately two thirds of the way through the original novel. The final third continues to demonstrate that "virtue" implies wisdom and generosity of spirit as well as prudence. Pamela must now face new temptations created by her lofty status, and the problems inherent in her sudden elevation. Her natural grace and intelligence prevail. She wins over the neighborhood gentry, and even, after some resistance, Lady Davers, Mr. B.'s haughty sister. She also succeeds in gaining the respect and affection of her former fellow servants, proving herself an admirable mistress of the household. She and her husband make prudent plans for her parents that will ensure them comfort and ease, but will not deprive them of their sense of independence, giving them a genuinely useful role to play in managing one of Mr. B.'s farms.

Perhaps the greatest test of Pamela's benevolence comes when she learns of her husband's illegitimate child. Mr. B. takes her to a country dairy where young girls from a nearby school come to breakfast as a special treat, and thus introduces her to Miss Goodwin, his "niece." Pamela is charmed by the child, and when she learns her true identity immediately suggests that she come to live with them. Mr. B., pleased that she shows no jealousy, tells her, "You are very good Pamela. And I have not once been deceived in the hopes my fond heart had entertained of your prudence" (434). Pamela's attitude toward the child's erring mother, Sally Godfrey, is even more generous, considering that she herself has resisted similar, if not greater, pressures from Mr. B. and might well adopt a tone of smug superiority. Miss Godfrey now lives virtuously in Jamaica after emigrating to escape the temptation of Mr. B.'s continuing solicitations. Pamela declares, "I honour her resolution," adding, "I should rank such a returning dear lady in the class of those who are most virtuous" (437). The final third of the book, then, does demonstrate the truth of Mr. B.'s assertion that "Pamela's *person,* all lovely as you see it, is far short of her *mind,*" and that while her beauty attracted him as a lover, it was "her mind that made me her *husband*" (364).

Eighteenth-century detractors focused chiefly on Richardson's moral

vision, but twentieth-century critics have also disparaged his craftsmanship, seeing his artistic achievement as the result of luck rather
than artistry. As we have seen above, Richardson quite consciously used
the technique of "writing to the moment" to secure the emotional involvement of his readers and thus make his exemplary characters more
effective. *Pamela* gives evidence of other literary devices as well, notably the recurrent use of clothing as a motif and the emblematic use of
landscape. The choice of clothing as a theme is particularly appropriate
for a novel whose protagonist is a fifteen year old. Detailed descriptions
of clothing not only form an index of Pamela's varying states of mind
but also realistically indicate one of the parameters of interest common
to most of those her age. The waistcoat that Pamela is embroidering
for Mr. B. in the first part of the novel becomes a barometer of her
attitude toward her employer, as well as the occasion for her staying in
the house. Pamela writes her parents, "Oh! I forgot to say, that I would
stay to finish the waistcoat, if I might with safety: Mrs. Jervis tells me
I certainly may," adding, "I never had a prettier piece of work" (31).
After further evidence of Mr. B.'s bad intentions, however, Pamela
writes, "I hope to have finished the ugly waistcoat in two days" (35).
Even more important is the use Richardson makes of Pamela's own
clothing in the novel. Shortly after the death of her mistress, Mr. B.
gives Pamela some of his mother's clothes. She sends her parents a
list—"A suit of my late lady's clothes, and half a dozen of her shifts,
and six fine handkerchiefs, and three of her cambric aprons, and four
Holland ones. The clothes are fine silk . . ." (7)—and, knowing they
may be suspicious of his kindness, reassures them that Mrs. Jervis was
present and that he gave the housekeeper clothing also. She is "sur-
prized at his goodness" and reports that "he gave these good things to
us with such a graciousness, as I thought he looked like an angel."
Here Pamela not only reveals her own unrecognized attraction to Mr.
B., but also describes an idealized situation—Mr. B., all angelic graciousness, dispensing only good things. His next gifts include some
stockings, and Pamela blushes awkwardly at receiving them from his
hands, but Mrs. Jervis reassures her that he is only giving her clothes
that will make her fit to be a personal maid to his sister, Lady Davers.
Her parents "hope there is not any thing in it," but caution her about
these "great favours" and about her finding him "so amiable and like
an angel" (9). After Mr. B.'s first advances in the garden, Pamela
thinks of leaving the house immediately, but, ironically, her fine
clothes are a hindrance, for "being pretty well dressed" she fears that

she "might come to some harm" (13). (Pamela's fears, which may seem foolish to a twentieth-century reader, are not groundless. Fine fabrics and clothing were very valuable, and even household linen left to dry outside was the target of thieves. Defoe's Moll Flanders acquires her underworld nickname from her skill in stealing expensive, imported fabrics from draper's shops.) She laments to her parents, "O how I wished for my gray russet again, and my poor dress with which you fitted me out" (13). As we have seen above, Pamela does make herself a new dress that will be suitable when she returns home, and the clothing is a sign of her cheerful acceptance of her fortune. When she appears in her country costume, neither Mrs. Jervis nor Rachel, the housemaid, recognize her at first, but when Mrs. Jervis manipulates a meeting between Mr. B. and the rustic "stranger," he knows her immediately. Unlike the others, Mr. B. sees beyond the immediate external signs of social class to the individual. It is this perception that makes it possible for him to marry Pamela at last.

Pamela continues to wear her new dress as a sign of her status. When Mr. B. asks her what she means by this, she tells him "I mean one of the honestest things in the world" (44), explaining that it is the fine clothes given her by her mistress which are a kind of disguise, because she came from her parents as a poor girl. The point is further emphasized when Pamela is about to return to her parents. As she packs up to leave she asks Mrs. Jervis to give her opinion of the justness of her proceedings, because she is determined to take with her "only what I can properly call my own" (63). Mrs. Jervis, without Pamela's knowledge, arranges that Mr. B. shall be a witness so that he will be convinced of her honesty. Pamela divides her possessions into three parcels. The first, she explains, were given her by her lady but she can have no claim to them now because they were intended to be worn in her mistress' service. The second she has still less right to for they were given by Mr. B. and they were meant to be the price of her shame. It is only the third parcel, "the companion of my poverty, and the witness of my honesty," that she will take with her. The scene does touch Mr. B., and persuades him that Pamela is not hypocritical. Ironically, it also increases his attraction to her, so that instead of letting her go to her parents he sends her to his Lincolnshire estate. During her captivity, Pamela continues to wear only her rustic clothes, even though Mr. B. sends trunks of fine clothes to her, but when their marriage is assured, she relates that she went up "and new dressed myself, taking possession, in a happy moment, I hope, of my *two bundles,* as my master was pleased to call them" (270). She gives a delighted catalog, telling that she "put on fine linen, silk shoes, and fine white cotton stockings, a fine quilted coat, a delicate green Mantua silk gown and coat, a French necklace, a laced cambric handkerchief, and clean gloves," and then, "taking my fan, I like a little proud hussy, looked in the glass, and thought myself a gentlewoman once more."

Richardson also uses landscape to give resonance to the themes of the novel. Pamela's first temptation, like Eve's, takes place in a garden. Unlike our first mother, however, Pamela staunchly resists. The garden of the Lincolnshire estate becomes a setting that helps to reveal the character of both Mr. B. and Pamela and to signify the vicissitudes of their relationship. The old-fashioned walled garden includes a plot for vegetables as well as more formal allées defined by high clipped hedges, and at its center a carp pond. It appears to Pamela first as a prison, with its high walls serving only to shut her in, but later it also seems to be a refuge, protecting her from external dangers. Pamela secures a key to the back gate from Mr. Williams, but when attempting her escape she is confronted by a "horrid bull, staring me full in the face with fiery saucer eyes, as I thought" (131). She later realizes, to her chagrin, that the bull is actually a meek cow, but she is restrained by other fears—"Then I know not one step of the way, nor how far to any house or cottage; and whether I could gain protection if I got to a house; And now the robbers are abroad too," and she concludes, "I may run into as great a danger as I want to escape" (132). Pamela's fears have a basis in reality—a housemaid has been gored by a bull and highwaymen were all too prevalent—but her hesitation also reflects her strong but unacknowledged attraction to Mr. B.

Early in her Lincolnshire captivity Pamela fishes in the carp pond. She catches a fish which she skillfully plays and brings to shore. But in that moment she sees the carp as a parallel to herself, also betrayed by false baits, and lets the fish go free. Later, as we have seen, the pond assumes a more sinister aspect when Pamela contemplates suicide. In terms of self-knowledge this scene is a turning point in the novel, revealing to Pamela the dangerous extent of her pride. It is the nadir of her fortunes, but it brings about renewal based upon trust rather than self-confidence. As Mr. B. moves toward his proposal of marriage, he sits beside her as she kneels on the sloping bank of the pond, takes her in his arms, and asks if he holds the first place in her heart. "And it was by the side of this pond, and not far from the place where I had that dreadful conflict, that my present hopes . . . began to dawn"

(187), Pamela tells us. He does finally propose to her in the garden, but Pamela, having been warned of a sham marriage, is afraid to accept. The lesson of trust has been well learned, however, and when Mr. B. sends after her she risks the consequences of a free return into his control. He then tells her, "I love you with a purer flame than ever I knew in my life, and which commenced for you in the garden" (236). In her new happiness all aspects of the garden are seen in a different light. Pamela reports on a walk with her father: "And with what delight, with what thankfulness, did we go over every scene . . . the fish-pond, the back-door and every place: O, what reason had we for thankfulness" (268).

The Lincolnshire garden is not only an index of Pamela's state of mind, but also emblematic of the ambiguities of Mr. B. himself. The eighteenth century was the great age of the natural or English garden. Following the lead of William Kent, who by using the ha-ha or sunken fence eliminated walls, opened up vistas and let it be seen that "all nature was a garden," the grounds of the great country houses were redesigned by Capability Brown and his followers. All over England Tudor gardens, characterized by encircling walls and formal allées, were redone in the new taste. Mr. B.'s garden, however, retains its old-fashioned character. He tells Pamela that the house was built in his great-grandfather's time, and the description of house and garden leads us to suspect that neither has been much altered. Early in the novel Pamela comments on Mr. B.'s filial piety, noting that "he was always dutiful to his parents" (2), and the pleasantly unfashionable nature of the garden suggests his fidelity to old values.

The garden is also relatively unpretentious. Pamela uses a homely sunflower as a marker for the hiding place where she leaves letters for Mr. Williams. She plays at gardening with still more homely horse beans to give her an excuse for digging in the loam to look for messages, and she sends an unsuspecting maid off to request a salad from the gardener to gain time to hide her letters. A severely manicured show piece would allow none of these activities. The allées, with their isolating walls of hedges, indicate the difficulties of Pamela's relationship with Mr. B. She has been summoned to join him in the garden, and she goes, noting, "how can I help being at his beck?" (211), but, seeing him in one walk, she deliberately takes another. Their paths eventually come together, however, and the episode concludes with their walking tenderly arm-in-arm, after he has just read in her journal the account of her near suicide.

The garden suggests old values, both for good and for bad—good in its evidence of regard for the past and its lack of gaudy show, but constricting also with its walls and closed vistas. The garden thus shows forth the character of its owner, Mr. B. He is essentially a man of the old mold. Before his reform he proceeds much in the tradition of *droit de seigneur,* and even after his reform he makes it clear that he will be a husband on the patriarchal model who demands absolute obedience from his wife. He recognizes that Pamela is, in fact, an ideal spouse for just this reason. He could not, he explains, have been happy if he "had wedded a fine lady, brought up pretty much in my own manner, and used to have her will in every thing" (403). The new style of companionate marriage at first has no appeal for Mr. B. who expects compliance, declaring, "and though I was not always right, that yet she would bear with me" (404).

Pamela, then, can certainly be defended against the charges of a narrow moral vision and lack of conscious artistry. It is, however, Richardson's first novel, written by his own account, in the incredibly short time of two months, in the midst of all his other business. Somewhat of an apprentice work, it does have flaws. Richardson thought that the appearance of verisimilitude was important in his fiction to secure the emotional involvement of readers that he saw as essential for his moral teaching. Knowing that fiction was held in low esteem, he felt that readers would more readily identify with a story that they thought was true. He wished to preserve "an *Air* of Genuineness" in order "to avoid hurting that kind of Historical Faith which Fiction itself is generally read with, tho' we know it to be Fiction."[15] *Pamela* was therefore published as a collection of real letters and there was, in fact, speculation at the time about the identity of the "real" Pamela. Richardson helps to establish the reality of the letters by using them to forward the plot. Much of Pamela's captivity is spent in trying to smuggle letters out of her prison, in hiding them, and in secreting supplies of paper and ink. Mr. B. has, in fact, stolen and intercepted some of her early letters to her parents, and in the end it is the reading of her letters that convinces him of Pamela's virtue, leading him to marry her. This structural use of the letters is highly artful, but Richardson sometimes stumbles when insisting unnecessarily on their probability. In the early part of the novel Pamela's absent parents provide a natural occasion for writing, and the close relationship between parents and child would encourage a full and detailed recounting of her actions. Nevertheless, Richardson sometimes protests too much. Letter 31, for example, is written at a time when Pamela expects to be with her parents within a day. The letter begins, "I will continue my writing still, because, may-be, I shall like to read it, when I am with you, to see what dangers I have been enabled to escape; although I bring it along with me" (71). Rather than reinforcing a sense of reality, this not only tends to remind the reader of the artificiality of the convention, but even to suggest that Pamela's letters are self-conscious rather than spontaneous. Pamela's letters become a journal during her captivity, and here the problem is more acute since she has no assurance that she will ever be able to transmit her writing to her parents. It is natural enough that the lonely girl would keep a diary as a defense against melancholy—adolescence is still the most usual time for journal writing—but, once again, Richardson's desire to authenticate the narrative sometimes serves only to emphasize its improbability. When Mr. B. arrives at the Lincolnshire estate, Pamela writes, "Good Sirs! good Sirs! What will become of me? Here is my master come in his fine chariot Indeed he is!—What shall I do? Where shall I hide myself?—O! What shall I do? Pray for me!" and then adds, "But O! you will not see this!" (159). The tension engendered by Richardson's technique of instantaneous description is broken by the unnecessary aside. On Pamela's wedding day she makes entries in her journal at six and eight-thirty in the morning, three in the afternoon, and then eight, ten, and eleven in the evening. Richardson tries to increase the probability of these frequent entries by having Pamela declare, "I have got such a knack of writing, that when by myself, I cannot sit without a pen in my hand" (306). Taken literally, this creates a ludicrous picture of neurotic compulsion, and the passage would be better omitted.

A more serious flaw in the novel is the character of Mr. B. Even though he can be defended against the charge of deep-dyed villainy, he remains a rather shallow and uninteresting character. He is highly egotistical, as Pamela herself recognizes. Shortly before the final reconciliation that leads to their marriage, she reflects, after a quarrel, "But see the lordliness of a high condition!—A poor body must not put in a word, when they take it in their heads to be angry! What a fine time a person of an equal condition would have of it, if she were to marry such a one," adding, "his poor dear mother spoiled him at first" (215). Lady Davers, his sister, later accedes to this judgment, declaring, "He is too lordly a creature by much; and can't bear disappointment, nor ever could" (399). His friends rally him "on the stateliness of his temper" and opine that the success of the marriage will depend on Pamela's meekness rather than "his complaisance." Mr. B. agrees, conceding that "in my conscience, I think I should have hardly made a tolerable [husband] to any but Pamela" (399). A degree of insular selfishness in Mr. B. is necessary to make his treatment of Pamela plausible, but the essentially egalitarian modern reader, who may not regard marriage into the aristocracy as supreme good fortune in itself, is apt to question whether Pamela's fate is truly a reward. This reservation then returns us to the question of Richardson's choice of a subtitle for the novel— *Pamela; or, Virtue Rewarded.* Even if virtue means more than physical chastity in the context of the novel, the equation suggested is overly simplistic, tending to locate the novel in the category of the romances that Richardson despised.

Some of the criticisms of the original *Pamela* Richardson sought to remedy in his sequel, which will be referred to here as *Pamela II.* He had not at first intended to write such a sequel, as the considerable portion of *Pamela I* that depicts the marriage indicates. The great popularity of the novel understandably created a powerful temptation for others to profit from it. Both anti-Pamelas and adaptations in the form of a heroic poem, plays, and a ballad opera soon appeared.[16] It was the threat, however, of a continuation by a hack, John Kelly, hired by the bookseller Chandler, that finally goaded Richardson into writing his own sequel. He explained to a friend that "rather than my Plan should be Ravished out of my Hands, and, probably my Characters depreciated and debased" he would continue the novel himself, although he considered it "Baseness as well as Hardship that a Writer could not be permitted to end his own Work, when and how he pleased, without such scandalous Attempts of Ingrafting upon his Plan."[17]

Pamela II is undoubtedly the least read and the most poorly regarded of Richardson's major works, and understandably so. The lack of a spontaneous creative impulse is all too apparent. The last third of the original *Pamela* becomes primarily a fictionalized conduct book, but momentum carries over from the earlier section, and the reader retains some curiosity to see how Pamela will cope with her new role. By the end of the original novel, she has demonstrated that she is fully capable of acting the part of Mrs. B., winning the approval of all. Although Richardson bravely maintained that there was ample material to fill his new volumes—"her Behaviour in Married Life, her Correspondences with her new and more genteel Friends; her Conversations at Table and elsewhere; her pregnant Circumstance, her Devotional and Charitable Employments . . ."[18]—the dramatic tension that made

Pamela I so effective is sadly lacking. Richardson's chief strength as a novelist is the delineation of interior conflict as characters confront important moral choices. As we have seen, the characterization of Mr. B. in *Pamela I* is flawed because the format of the book does not permit readers to participate in his struggles of conscience as he pursues Pamela. In *Pamela II* this flaw persists, Pamela is still virtually the only letter writer, and the damage is greater because Pamela herself has no important choices to make. In the most important conflict of the book, her problem is more one of decorum than of deciding between right and wrong. Symptomatic of the lower intensity of the sequel is the nature of Pamela's letters. In the first novel Pamela writes to her parents, confiding all her thoughts without disguise or pretention. In *Pamela II* she writes to Lady Davers, her imperious sister-in-law, with the understanding that her letters will be shared by "my lord and the earl . . . , and the Countess, and Lady Betty" (23). Pamela, in agreeing to the correspondence, notes that "you must not expect, that I can entirely divest myself of that awe which will necessarily lay me under a greater restraint, than if writing to my parents" (36). Even her letters to Polly Darnford, a young woman her own age, are not confidences between friends since they are also "to oblige your honoured mama, and your good neighbors" (89). The air of artless spontaneity so characteristic of the earlier work is necessarily lost.

Mr. B.'s entanglement with a countess provides the one suspenseful episode in this book. Pamela is persuaded, against her will, to go to a masquerade, a popular entertainment at the time. Although sometimes private, masquerades were often subscription balls where for the price of the admission ticket pleasure seekers could enjoy not only the usual diversions of music and dancing but also the thrill of anonymous flirtation. These balls were universally condemned by moralists, and frequently provided novelists of the century with the occasion for misadventures on the part of the heroine. Mr. B. has chosen for Pamela the decorous guise of a Quaker, while he assumes the more dashing costume of a Spanish don. When he is singled out by a bold nun who talks Italian to him, Pamela observes that the lady certainly does not keep to the character of her costume. The nun continues to haunt Mr. B. until Pamela, disliking the freedoms that masks permit and uneasy with the flirtatious behavior of the mysterious stranger, feigns illness to force departure. She is pregnant at the time, and her attention is soon engaged in caring for her newly born son. Her friend Polly Darnford, however, learns not only that the nun is the young Countess

Dowager of ————, a widow noted for her lack of reserve, but that she is corresponding with Mr. B. Soon, rumors begin to fly. Pamela, striving to act the part of the perfect wife, gives no voice to her suspicions. She tries to find consolation in the nursery, but she is all too apt to greet Mr. B. with tear-swollen eyes and weak attempts at a smile. Annoyed, he attributes her "vapourish" behavior to exaggerated maternal solicitude, and chides her with being quite altered with "strange melancholy airs" (292).

Tension mounts between the couple, until finally Pamela stages her "trial." She appears before a bar, formed by the backs of three chairs, and Mr. B. sitting as judge. Acknowledging the superior charms of the countess, she asks only to be allowed to take Billy, their child, to live with her at her parents' house in Kent, confessing that she cannot "divide my interest in you, knowingly, with any lady on earth" (312). Mr. B., touched, assures her that although he has indeed been "inconsiderately led on by blind passion," it is still in his power to "restore to your virtue a husband all your own" (314). In fact, he tells Pamela that from now on she will be his tutelary angel, and he will obey her dictates. The affair, he explains, began through a love of intrigue coupled with pride and vanity in having succeeded in attracting so desirable a woman. The beautiful young widow agreed to defy the opinion of a censorious world by demonstrating the possibility of a purely platonic friendship. Then, when he saw Pamela continually solemn and tearful, in contrast to the lively countess, he found a further excuse for seeking pleasure away from a home which was becoming irksome. As the malicious gossip of the town proclaimed them guilty and as Pamela's jealousy became more apparent, he was beginning to be tempted to make his imputed guilt a reality. Now, after the "trial," he sees that "Platonic love is Platonic nonsense" (323), and, his love for Pamela reaffirmed, their marriage is stronger than ever, with Mr. B. declaring, "I always *loved* you, my dearest . . . but I *revere* you now" (318).

Such an episode, one might think, could well provide enough emotional tension to power an entire novel. However, Richardson's treatment of it dissipates this potential energy. Pamela herself, aside from the initial encounter at the masquerade, is an outsider, learning of events at secondhand. She deliberately avoids any confrontation, and instead of dramatic scenes we see only a red-eyed Pamela and an irritable Mr. B., both skirting the truth. She remains passive, taking comfort in her own virtue and consoling herself with the company of her beloved infant. Summarizing her prospects, if she is allowed to take the baby to live with her parents, she explains that she will "enjoy a two-fold happiness, that of doing my own duty to my dear baby—a pleasing entertainment this! and that of comforting my worthy parents and being comforted by them—a no small consolation!" (288). Although grief-stricken at the loss of her husband's love, she will have the recompense of gaining merit in heaven, for nothing, she determines, will "rob me of the merit of a patient sufferer" (293). In fact, as she herself admits, she will be much better off than she once hoped to be with "her virtue and good name secured," with herself and her parents "bountifully provided for" (302), and with the joy of her infant son. Pamela's plight does engage the reader's interest, but her situation is not truly pathetic.

While Pamela adopts a quiescent role, Mr. B. makes the active moves. The reader, however, never participates in his decisions or experiences his temptations, hesitations, and moral debate. We are as much in the dark as Pamela, seeing him as a remote and querulous tyrant. Finally, we learn the complete story, but only retrospectively and only at secondhand through Pamela's report of his revelations. The materials for an account of inner struggle that would involve the reader emotionally are ample. Mr. B., flattered by the countess's notice and conscious of his own restraint, becomes increasingly annoyed with Pamela's tearful mien, fearing that her temperament has entirely changed, perhaps because of her absorbing concern for the new baby. As duty combined with love pulls him toward Pamela, jealousy of her attentiveness to the child and the manifold attractions of the countess pull him away. The countess's uncle nastily suggests that a man who married beneath himself may now want to prove himself by seducing a lady of birth. The slur is vigorously denied by both Mr. B. and the countess, but certainly a beautiful and high-born mistress is a temptation to the ego. Richardson's most effective subject, "the divided heart," could be exemplified as Mr. B.'s pride wars with his sense of duty and his belief in platonic friendship begins to yield to sensual desire. This, with the contrapuntal theme of Pamela's own exaggerated fears, would create real drama, but the reader is not allowed to participate actively in this struggle through an account written "to the moment." Even Pamela's anxiety is not chronicled in an effective way. Her letters are written principally to Lady Davers, Mr. B.'s sister, a recipient to whom Pamela would naturally be reluctant to confide her suspicions, and in all her letters she is careful to maintain wifely decorum, avoiding any display of dirty linen in public.

In place of presenting real conflict, Richardson's sequel chiefly gives lessons in conduct. Some of the incidents are designed to counter criticisms of the original novel. The "warm" scenes in *Pamela,* depicting Mr. B.'s abortive attempts on her virtue, were criticized as being unnecessarily inflaming, but when Lady Davers is allowed to read all of Pamela's letters she vigorously defends these passages, pointing out that unless one knew all the facts one could not fully appreciate Pamela's merit nor could proper justice be done to Mr. B. through realizing that "he was not so very abandoned, but he could stop short of the execution of his wicked purposes" (28). Furthermore, she maintains, there are "no scenes but such as make his wickedness odious: and that gentleman, much more lady, must have a very corrupt heart, who could . . . make any reflections, but what should be to your honour" (27). Even the rakish Jackey, she assures Pamela, evinced only the most appropriate reactions. Fielding, among others, also claimed that *Pamela* encouraged young gentlemen to marry their mother's maids and enjoined chambermaids to look out for their masters, teaching them the little arts necessary for that purpose. In *Pamela II* Richardson shows by the beginnings of an affair between Lord Jackey, Lady Davers' foolish nephew, and Polly Barlow, Pamela's maid, that the marriage of Pamela and Mr. B. is not necessarily a pattern to be imitated. Polly is no Pamela. When she discovers Polly allowing compromising caresses, Pamela points out, "I was once in as dangerous a situation as you can be in. And I did not escape it, child, by the language and conduct I heard from you" (187). Nor is Lord Jackey a Mr. B. Pamela is almost as annoyed by Polly's poor choice as she is by her transgression. "What a wretch art thou" (194), she thinks, considering for what a poor creature Polly is willing to sacrifice her virtue, "Thou art sunk indeed! Too low for excuse, and almost beneath pity!" (195). In contrast, Mr. B. is increasingly revealed as an exceptional man, while Pamela continues to exemplify the ideal woman.

Some admirers of the original novel, Alexander Pope, for example, suggested that Richardson use the sequel as an opportunity to comment on London society in all its artificiality through the wondering eyes of Pamela, an unsophisticated newcomer. The masquerade, together with a few scenes at the theater and other fashionable places of resort, does follow this format but without using the sharply satiric tone that Pope undoubtedly hoped for. Richardson was probably unwilling to make his heroine into the traditional wide-eyed ingenue, the naif of satire, that would make such a plan most effective. Instead, the novel is chiefly concerned with domestic scenes, with the daily life of Pamela and her husband, and it thereby becomes a marriage manual. As such, it suggests a pattern for marriage radically different from the standard conduct books popular at the time, and in fact, from the advice given in *Familiar Letters*. These works, such as *The Ladies' Calling*, usually attributed to Richard Allestree, or *The Lady's New-Year's Gift* by "a Father," counseled complete obedience and passive acceptance on the part of the wife. She must never question either her husband's judgment or his actions. Criticizing his decisions, even in her secret thoughts, was not merely impolitic but morally wrong. If a wife suspected infidelity, she was advised never openly to accuse her husband, but to continue to act as if nothing had happened.

This, of course, is the role that Pamela does follow at first, but Mr. B. makes it clear that she would have done far better to ignore the conduct books. She should have stated her fears openly, since he, conscious of his own innocence and ignorant of the tales informers have forced upon Pamela, was simply puzzled and irritated by her apparently causeless melancholy. When she excused her lack of gaiety by citing worries over minor nursery crises, she only made Mr. B. jealous of his own son. The frank avowal that finally results from Pamela's "trial" comes just in time to save Mr. B. from actual infidelity, but it could have come much sooner if Pamela had rejected the code prescribed by conduct books.

In one important decision, Mr. B. does demand obedience and Pamela does submit, although reluctantly. She wishes to nurse the baby, holding that it is a natural duty and therefore divinely ordained. Mr. B., however, replies that not only does he value her "genteel form" but, more importantly, he takes pleasure in her companionship and does not welcome "even a son and heir" (229) as his rival when "baby offices . . . better benefit weaker minds." A final argument is that she is not robust and may injure her health. Pamela declares that she must be the judge since she will be called to account and must rise or fall by her own actions. In countering this argument, Mr. B. invokes the principle of coverture, maintaining "that if a wife thinks a thing her duty to do, which her husband does not approve, he can dispense with her performing it, and no sin shall lie at her door" (202). Under eighteenth-century law husband and wife were considered one person. The wife's property was therefore controlled by her husband and she could not legally sign contracts or engage in any binding transactions. One curious feature of this doctrine was that the wife also could not be

considered guilty of any action performed in the presence of or with
the express consent of her husband. A wife, in theory, could kill a man
and if her husband was present he would incur the legal guilt. Mr. B.
is transferring this concept to the moral realm. Pamela writes to her
parents, hoping that they will support her cause, but her father replies
that while they regret Mr. B.'s stance, she should acquiesce when he
"thinks so highly of his prerogative," citing the laws of the realm
which "excuse a wife when she is faulty by the command of her husband" (232). Pamela does then yield, although it "was a point of conscience to me" (235).

The usual pattern in their relationship, however, in contradiction to
the marriage manuals, is that of mutual consultation and decision making. Mr. B. has been notably willful since childhood, and, as we have
seen above, friends and relatives alike consider it fortunate that he has
chosen a wife who will be meek and compliant. Pamela first attempts
to influence her husband's behavior (in *Pamela I*) when she intercedes
in a quarrel between him and his sister, Lady Davers. Her mild re-
monstrances provoke a full-scale temper tantrum that is followed by a
list of forty-eight rules to be observed in her conduct toward him,
including, "I must not, when he is in great wrath with anybody, break
in upon him without his leave" and "I must bear with him even when
I find him in the wrong" (407). As Pamela comments, much of this
"looks a little hard, methinks! This would bear a small debate, I fancy,
in a parliament of women" (408). In the beginning, then, their marriage is indeed in the authoritarian, patriarchal mode so often advocated in conduct books, but in *Pamela II* Mr. B.'s attitude changes. "I
always intend, my dear, you shall judge for yourself," he now tells
Pamela, "if you have anything on your mind to say, let's have it; for
your arguments are always new and unborrowed" (168–69). When she
fears that she may have spoken too freely about some of his friends, he
assures her, "I never, my love, ask you a question I wish you not to
answer; and always expect your answer should be without reserve,"
adding, "for many times I may ask your opinion as a corrective or a
confirmation of my own judgment" (227). He chides her when, rather
than speaking out, she shows her reservations by "bashful seriousness,"
telling her, "never *hesitate* to me your consent in anything" (155), explaining that he will conform to her wishes if he finds them reasonable,
and always wants to know her judgment. On one occasion, Pamela
uses feminine wiles to get her way rather than a direct and reasoned
approach. "And have you thus come over me, Pamela!", Mr. B. ex-

claims, "Go, I am half angry with you, for leading me on in this manner against myself," and reproaches her for surprising him "by art." He counsels her, "your talent is nature, and you should keep to that!" (279). Their relations are to be the open and candid exchanges of equals, not the manipulative stratagems and subterfuges character-istic of the wheedling wife. In reflecting on the affair with the countess and resolving on a new course of life, Mr. B. makes his most sweeping renunciation of husbandly privilege. "And now, my Pamela, from this instant you shall be my guide," he declares, "I will leave it to you to direct as you please" (423).

Mr. B.'s actions support his declarations of equality. Pamela has been quite well educated, according to the standards of the period, by her late mistress, mastering higher feminine accomplishments, such as playing the spinet and fine needlework, as well as the more basic sub-jects. After her marriage, however, Mr. B. delights in instructing her further, Pamela records, not only in French, Italian, and Latin, but in the fine discriminations of poetry, pictures, and medals, encouraging her curiosity and finding that her observations improve his own judg-ment. He also takes Pamela on the grand tour, the traditional final educational polish for young men of the period. Finally he shows his confidence in her abilities by giving her John Locke's treatise on edu-cation to read and entrusting her with directing the education of their children. One precept of Locke gains Pamela's complete approval and she quotes it at length: "But under whose care soever a child is put to be taught, during the tender and flexible years of his life, this is cer-tain, it should be one who thinks Latin and language the least part of education" (409). Knowledge of Latin was the chief advantage of ed-ucated men in the century. Women were usually not permitted to study Latin or Greek because it would be too great a strain for their frail intellects, and then denied any claim to participation in intelli-gent discourse because they did not know classical languages. In de-claring that "I have long had the thought, that much time is wasted to little purpose in the attaining of Latin" (409), Pamela is really af-firming the parity of women, despite their supposedly defective education.

Pamela decries the education customarily meted out to women, not-ing that "We are forced to struggle for knowledge," and "when a poor girl, in spite of her narrow education, breaks out into notice, her ge-nius is immediately tamed by trifling employments." Her own case is different, however, she tells her husband, because "you, Sir, act more nobly with your Pamela; for you throw in her way all opportunities of improvement" (386). Miss Goodwin, her young ward, is already a perfect mistress of French, is familiar with the best characters in the *Spectators,* and is beginning the study of both Latin and Italian. Pamela notes that Locke advocates mothers teaching their children, but asks, "And who, I pray, as our sex is generally educated, shall teach the *mothers?*" (413). Disparaging the excessive time spent by girls in embroidering samplers and doing other "unnecessary things," she declares that girls should be entitled to the same education as boys, differing only in play and diversions. Then, she asserts, they will "direct their inclinations to useful subjects, such as would make them above the imputations of some unkind gentlemen, who allot to their part common tea-table prattle, while they do all they can to make them fit for nothing else, and then upbraid them for it" (413).

Rational companionship is seen as the ideal for all couples. When Polly Darnford is offered the wealthy and titled Lord Jackey as a spouse, she declines on the grounds that her "husband must be a man of sense." Women who encourage the conventional romantic rhetoric instead of sounding out suitors through intelligent conversation are apt to find "a strange and shocking difference" when "fond lovers, prostrate at their feet" are transformed into "surly husbands trampling upon their necks" (438). Far from males being the superior sex, Pamela concludes, after assessing virtually all the couples they know, that "notwithstanding the disparity of education and the difference in the opportunities of each" the women "make *more* than an equal figure with the gentlemen" (415).

The more normal milieu of *Pamela II* allowed Richardson to explore a greater variety of social situations than the restricted settings of the original novel permitted. In the sequel he experimented with new characters, sketched new plots, and sharpened his skill in dialogue. With the use of hindsight, we can see much of this as trial runs that would be more fully developed in *Clarissa* and *Sir Charles Grandison.*

Polly Darnford is the most engaging new character to appear. She is witty and independent, often chafing at the role women are by custom obliged to play. Miss Darnford strongly resembles Anna Howe, Clarissa's friend, and, like Anna, she also provides a confidant for the protagonist. Richardson does not, unfortunately, make full use of her in this role, although candid letters to Polly Darnford would have brought greater vividness to Pamela's travail over the countess. In *Clarissa* he will fully exploit the possibilities of such a companionship.

Polly's relations with her sister, Nancy, also prefigure Clarissa's with her sister, Bella. In this case Polly, the elder, is more attractive, intelligent, and better-humored than her younger sister, Nancy. This comparison will hold in *Clarissa,* with the respective ages reversed. It is Polly who attracts numerous suitors while her sister looks on enviously, until Mr. Murray, refused by Polly, then courts Nancy. Polly explains to Pamela that she hopes her rather boorish beau "will be easily persuaded to quit me for Nancy; for I see he has not delicacy enough to love with any great distinction" (88). She paints an amusing picture of how her sister "screwed up her mouth" and declared "she'd have none of Polly's leavings" until Mr. Murray made a direct declaration to her whereupon "the *gaudy wretch,* as he was before with her, became a *well-dressed* gentleman" and "the *chattering magpie* (for he talks and laughs much), *quite conversable*" (121). Some lively bickering ensues between the sisters and Nancy sketches a scenario, here untrue, that Richardson later actually used to terminate Lovelace's unwilling courtship of Bella. Mr. Murray, she declares, quickly seized a coy denial from Polly in order to turn his affections to the younger sister, his real love. "Don't be angry, sister," she patronizingly advises, "that he took you at the first word" (175).

Sir Jacob Swynford, Mr. B.'s uncle, might serve as a partial model for Clarissa's father. "He is an absolute tyrant in his family," we are told, having disallowed the courtships of his children for selfish reasons, "and he seemed to please himself how much they stood in awe of him" (173). In *Pamela II,* however, Sir Jacob is primarily seen as a foolish figure of fun. He has declared his adamant opposition to Mr. B.'s marriage and his unwillingness to countenance a "cottage" bride by even meeting her. When the assembled company play a trick on him, introducing Pamela as the Countess of C.'s youngest daughter, he finds her "a charming creature" and regrets that his nephew had not met this lovely lady before marrying a low-born wench. The comedy continues until Pamela, in her disguise, chides him for sowing "seeds of indifference and animosity between man and wife" and trying to make Mr. B. dissatisfied with his choice. Sir Jacob finally agrees to meet Mr. B.'s wife, and on discovering the truth is thoroughly ashamed of himself. Sir Jacob's actions, the countess declares, are an "instance of stupid pride and churlishness" that brings "ridicule upon the pride of descent" (164).

The character of Lovelace is faintly foreshadowed in the report of a noble libertine who courts Miss Cope, a young lady of nineteen. When her parents forbid him the house and forbid their daughter to receive any attentions from him, he plots to elope with her "out of the private garden door," so that having "triumphed over her innocence" he can "revenge himself on the daughter, for the disgrace he had received from the parents" (440). The story is by no means parallel since Miss Cope is described as foolishly susceptible, but one of Lovelace's motivations is his desire to humiliate the Harlowe family for their rejection of his courtship.

Some scenes depict witty exchanges, as in Pamela's repartee with admiring fops at the masquerade, and many recount general social exchange that illuminates subtleties of manner and decorum. As in the novels of Jane Austen, manners are seen as the reflection of morals. Pamela's actions are always truly polite because she truly shows forth Christian values, while the behavior of some of the aristocrats, such as Sir Jacob, is seen as coarse and brutal, mirroring their own inner defects. Pamela in her own household creates a world that embodies real goodness, not merely in daily household prayers but in the consideration shown by and to each member of it. Richardson was to further elaborate this ideal of a Christian utopia in *Sir Charles Grandison*.

Pamela, Richardson's first novel, has considerable strengths but also some flaws. It is the apprentice work of a great novelist. The sequel, lacking the characteristic intensity of Richardson's best work, is of interest primarily in its depiction of a model marriage. This description will be further developed in Richardson's last novel *Sir Charles Grandison*.

Chapter Three
Clarissa

Clarissa is Richardson's greatest novel, a complex work of subtle artistry. While *Pamela* was written very quickly, *Clarissa* occupied Richardson for perhaps five years, the last year and a half spent in revising and trying to shorten the manuscript.[1] He retained all the strengths of *Pamela* but avoided the formal problems of his first novel, developing new techniques that enabled him to present characters with unrivaled depth and subtlety. In *Pamela*, Richardson created a heroine who could attain happiness by adhering to virtuous conduct, and a rake who could flout the conventions of his society to find true fulfillment. In *Clarissa*, the picture is darker. Richardson develops two remarkable protagonists, Clarissa and Lovelace, who are destroyed by the false values of the world each inhabits—Clarissa because she defies her world, Lovelace because he is trapped in his. Instead of the comforting simplicity of "Virtue Rewarded" he presents the anguish of a struggle to live according to a truly moral standard while contending with inner conflict and outer pressures. In his depiction of the workings of the consciousness, the growth of self-awareness, and the minute discriminations demanded of his heroine, Richardson achieved a level of psychological realism that would not be attempted again until the twentieth century.

The chief difficulties in *Pamela*, as we saw in the previous chapter, arose from the use of Pamela as the sole letter writer. In *Clarissa*, Richardson expanded his format, creating two principal pairs of writers—Clarissa and Anna Howe, Lovelace and Belford—as well as numerous minor writers—Clarissa's family, Mrs. Norton, the pedantic clergyman Brand, the servant Joseph Leman, and so forth. Thus, while Mr. B. remained a shadowy figure to the reader, seen only through Pamela's eyes, Lovelace becomes a fascinating character whom we experience through his own letters written "to the moment," exploring his plans and hesitations, his doubts and justifications, his beliefs and fantasies. The double correspondence also permits a fuller exploration of motives and self-knowledge as Anna Howe probes her friend's expressed statements for concealed meanings, forcing her to examine her feelings more closely. These multiple correspondences place an even greater burden on the reader to be an active participant in the novel. Not only does the reader observe the characters struggling to understand each other, but also to interpret the very text of the novel—that is, the letters themselves. The reader sometimes has a privileged position that enables him, for example, to see the dramatic irony in Clarissa's satisfaction with her prudent choice of lodgings in London. (The reader knows she has fallen into Lovelace's carefully baited trap.) But often the reader knows very little more than Clarissa herself, and, therefore, lacking the guidance of an omniscient narrator, reads the text, the letters, with the same anxious attention that the characters themselves read them. Richardson did skillfully incorporate Pamela's writing into the development of the novel itself, and it is her letters that bring about Mr. B.'s final capitulation, but in *Clarissa* he exploits the full ambiguity of the letter as a form in order to involve the reader in a continuous task of interpretation. The letter, as Christina Marsden Gillis has pointed out,[2] is basically a private document but, paradoxically, depends upon a reader to fulfill its purpose. Eighteenth-century readers familiar with, for example, the pirating of Pope's letters and then the subsequent "authentic" version that gave grounds for suspicion of editing, would be well aware of the possible ambiguities inherent even in collections of "real" letters. Furthermore, every private letter is the product of a particular writing in a delimited situation that must be evaluated by the recipient. Truthfulness to actual facts can never be assumed, if only because fallible humans are not omniscient. Richardson's form, then, encourages the reader to question and to form judgments; "It is not an unartful Management to interest the Readers so much in the Story as to make them differ in Opinion,"[3] he wrote, and even declared that his novels could be seen as "Trials of the Reader's Judgement, Manners, Taste, Capacity."[4] His method, he noted, made his readers "if not Authors, Carvers,"[5] that is, participants rather than passive receivers.

As in *Pamela,* the plot of *Clarissa* is relatively simple. Clarissa, the youngest child of a prosperous merchant family, is courted by Lovelace, an aristocratic rake. James Harlowe, Clarissa's brother, personally dislikes Lovelace, who outshone him at Oxford, and fears that Clarissa's marriage into the aristocracy will lead his wealthy bachelor uncles to will their estates to her rather than to him. Clarissa has already inherited her grandfather's estate. Bella, Clarissa's sister, is not only jealous of her beauty and accomplishments but also furious at having lost Lovelace as a suitor for herself. Using Lovelace's libertine reputation as their chief weapon, they unite the family—an authoritarian, patriarchal father, a weak and passive mother, the crusty, harsh uncle Antony, and the more mild uncle John—into opposition to Lovelace, and propose an alternative—Solmes. Solmes is a repulsive, mean-spirited vulgarian whose estates conveniently adjoin Clarissa's. He promises munificent settlements as well as the reversion of all his estates to the Harlowes if there should be no heir. In addition, he will exchange some of his land with James to increase the value of the estates James already holds. As Clarissa comments, James's "darling view" is that of *"raising a family, as it is called,"* that is, of acquiring a position substantial enough to permit "great substance" to be complemented with "rank and title."[6] The acquisition of titles by wealthy merchant families was, in fact, a commonplace of the times.

Clarissa asserts that she cannot marry a man whom she can neither love nor respect. Her father declares that he *will* be obeyed. James and Bella foment discord, as does, unknown to them, Joseph Leman, a servant suborned by Lovelace. Clarissa, hoping to avoid further violence after James fights a duel with Lovelace, has continued to correspond with Lovelace, at first with her mother's consent. Pressure mounts in the Harlowe household, and a forced marriage to the detestable Solmes seems imminent. Clarissa, desperate, accepts Lovelace's offer of help. At the last minute she changes her mind, but she is nevertheless tricked by Lovelace's stratagems into running away.

Now Clarissa is seen by the world as having eloped with a libertine. Abandoned by her family, cursed by her father, separated from her only friend, and imprisoned in Sinclair's brothel, Clarissa engages in a lonely duel with Lovelace. As in *Pamela,* at stake is the question of whose code of values will triumph. Clarissa is truly Christian, holding beliefs founded in trust, generosity, and mutual respect. Lovelace subscribes to the code of the rake that sees women as an inferior sort of creation, essentially corrupt, hypocritically restrained only by an artificial code imposed by society, and therefore fair game for deception and sexual conquest. Unable to overcome Clarissa by any other means, Lovelace eventually drugs and rapes her, convinced that "once subdued always subdued."

The result demonstrates how little Lovelace has understood Clarissa. Now convinced of his absolute villainy, Clarissa, far from being abashed or shamed, treats him with the contempt he deserves. She

rejects all offers to mitigate his guilt by marriage, declaring, *"The man who has been the villain to me you have been, shall never make me his wife"* (3:222). She manages to escape from him, finds humble lodgings, and, in failing health, prepares for a Christian death. Her family remains intransigent until too late, and then bitterly mourns her. Lovelace, despite Clarissa's specific prohibition of vengeance, is killed in a duel by her cousin Morden.

Clarissa is a novel of great length as well as complexity, so it is helpful to divide the work into three parts for the purpose of discussion. This, in fact, reflects the publication of the original volumes that appeared in three installments: volumes 1–2, volumes 3–4, and volumes 5–7. Volume 2 ends with Anna's first letter to Clarissa after the elopement, and volume 4 concludes just before the rape with Lovelace preparing to trick Clarissa back to Sinclair's.

The focus of the first part of the novel, the events leading up to Clarissa's running away with Lovelace, is the confrontation between Clarissa and her family. In this portion we become well acquainted with Clarissa and her friend Anna Howe, as well as with the Harlowe family. We meet Lovelace, but our knowledge of him is, by comparison, slight, and he writes few of the letters in this first part. The emphasis here is upon the conduct of the Harlowes as their greed and hunger for power reveal the hypocrisy of their commitment to a truly moral code of conduct. The indictment of the Harlowes is a condemnation of the accepted values of the society Richardson lived in where nominal virtue was often a disguise for rapacity or, at best, indifference to other human beings. Women were particularly vulnerable in this Hobbesian world of conflict and aggression. As daughters they were commodities to be disposed of advantageously; as wives their chief virtue was submissiveness. Clarissa echoes the plight of many as she pleads, "Only leave me myself" (1:399).

The novel begins on a note of characteristic urgency with Anna Howe asking for an account of the "disturbances that have happened in your family" (11). Richardson's new format of dual correspondences allows Anna to speak of her friend's merits, avoiding the problem of self-praise that plagued *Pamela,* and to give an objective view of the duel between James Harlowe and Lovelace, to the credit of the latter, a description that it would not be suitable for Clarissa herself to write. Letters between Clarissa and Anna dominate the first portion of the novel. The interaction between the two correspondents gives Richardson opportunities not only to present different points of view, and, as

Clarissa increasingly becomes a prisoner, to provide some objective assessment from the outside world, but also to allow Anna to question her friend, to probe her feelings and motives, and, in a certain sense, to act as a surrogate for the reader. Here, Anna's wish to know the background of the quarrel produces a summary of the events leading up to it.

Lovelace has been first introduced into the family through Uncle Antony as a suitor for Arabella at a time when Clarissa was away from home. We later learn from Lovelace that he actually sought Clarissa, having heard of her reputation for virtue, beauty, and wit, but was presented with the wrong sister. He quickly demonstrates his talent for strategy and manipulation by maneuvering Bella into a situation where the courtship customs of the day compel her to refuse his proposal, proffered when she is angry. Her denial, intended to be merely protocol, is taken as final, and Lovelace paves the way for his future courtship of Clarissa by expressing his regret at not being allied to a family he deeply respects. He has, however, now earned the enmity of the discarded Bella who soon finds an ally when James returns from Scotland. James already envies Lovelace for his personal qualities, and, more importantly, fears him as an economic threat if he marries Clarissa. While James, Bella, and the whole Harlowe family now adopt a virtuous pose, cantingly condemning Lovelace for his faulty morals, it is clear that for them marriage is a mercantile bargain that ignores spiritual claims. For Clarissa, on the other hand, marriage is a sacrament, a sacred bond that will shape not only her life in this world but her chance of salvation. The fundamental outlook of the Harlowes is so different from that of Clarissa, that it leads to real misunderstanding. From their viewpoint her protests are simply pious posturings that conceal a hidden motive, while she is constantly puzzled at what seems to her unnatural behavior from those who should love her best.

In the Harlowes Richardson created a paradigm of the evils that underlaid the accepted social values of the age. In Clarissa's father we see patriarchy embodied. Ironically, his wealth is largely due to his wife's dowry and inheritance, but despite, or perhaps because of, this he insists upon absolute command. James and Bella are clever enough to manipulate him into seeing the conflict with Clarissa in very simple terms. "Be assured of this," he tells Mrs. Norton, Clarissa's former nurse, "we will not be baffled by her. We will not appear like fools in this matter, and as if we had no authority over our own daughter" (1:192). Clarissa's uncles are also brought to see the question almost

entirely in terms of authority, although family pride strongly seconds
this position. While Clarissa's father has improved his position through
marrying wealth, Uncle John has made his money from mines, and
harsh Uncle Antony has amassed his fortune in the East India Company. In the brothers Richardson provides a schema of eighteenth-century routes to upward mobility. While Clarissa's marriage into the
aristocracy would be pleasing, still more pleasing is James's plan of
aggrandizing his own position. This, Clarissa's mother exclaims, is "a
plan that captivates us all: and a family so rich in all its branches, and
that has its views to honour, must be pleased to see a very great probability of taking rank one day among the principal in the kingdom"
(1:87). Clarissa herself is the trading commodity necessary to complete
their "darling view," and, in her family's eyes, Lovelace is the enemy
who has the power to gainsay them. The uncles, like Clarissa's father,
also translate her struggle into terms they can easily understand and
justify—a male contention for victory. Uncle John explains, "We are
resolved to frustrate him, and triumph over him, rather than he should
triumph over us: that's one word for all" (1:155). James, of course,
needs no persuasion that his sister should be sacrificed for his advantage. "Daughters," in his view, are "but encumbrances and drawbacks
upon a family . . . chickens brought up for the tables of other men"
(1:54). Women in general are contemptible to him, designed only for
humble servitude. "I know not what wit in a woman is good for," says
James, "but to make her over-value herself, and despise every other
person" (1:138).

Envy enlists Arabella's voice on the side of the Harlowe males, while
the mother's voice has long been stilled in family councils. In Clarissa's
parents we see the result of following conventional conduct book advice
on marriage. Clarissa's mother, as such tracts enjoined, has yielded her
will on all occasions to her irascible husband, despite the fact that, on
the testimony of both Anna Howe and Lovelace as well as Clarissa, she
is his superior in intelligence, in birth (she is a viscount's daughter)
and, originally, in wealth. Her submissive behavior has earned her only
contempt. Anna Howe laments that she has "long behaved unworthy
of her birth and fine qualities in yielding so much" only to find that
"it always produced a strength in the will of others . . . which subjected her to an arbitrariness that of course grew, and became estab-
lished" (1:130–31). Even Clarissa, reluctant to criticize her mother,
confides to Anna, "For if I may say to you, my dear, what I would not
to any other person living, it is my opinion that had she been of a

temper that would have bourne less, she would have had ten times less to bear than she has had" (1:22). Aunt Hervey's role in decision making is subservient not only because she is a woman but because she has not married well and is "perhaps under some little obligation" (1:60), while Clarissa's former nurse, Mrs. Norton, "a woman deserving of all consideration for her wisdom," is excluded because of "not being wealthy enough to have due weight" (1:60–61).

The customary understanding between parents and children was, as outlined in chapter 1, that a child would never marry without parental consent but that parents would never force a child to marry against his, or more often her, will. Clarissa tries in vain to get her family to abide by this compact. She not only pledges never to marry without their consent but never to marry at all, and to give up her estate. "Will not this be accepted?" Clarissa asks. "Surely it must" (1:306), she believes, but it is not. The refusal is based upon several considerations. First, the Harlowes are afraid that "the eyes of the world" will judge them as harsh persecutors, but, more importantly, they believe that Clarissa's refusal of Solmes can only be grounded in a preference for Lovelace, a preference to which she will inevitably yield and then empower Lovelace, as her husband, to contest the estate. Clarissa's cry, "Only leave me *myself*" (1:399), goes unheeded because she lives in a world where she is not an individual but a token in a game of power in which men are the only real players.

Richardson makes clear that Clarissa's situation is not to be seen as wholly exceptional or as resulting only from the malice of James and Bella. Mrs. Howe, Anna's mother, and Mrs. Norton each give a clear presentation of the conflict as seen by well meaning bystanders. Mrs. Howe's position is summarized by her daughter Anna: "Either, said she, the lady must be thought to have very violent inclinations (and what nice young creature would have that supposed?) which she *could* not give up; or a very stubborn will, which she *would* not; or, thirdly, have parents she was indifferent about obliging" (1:293). She amplifies this, explaining that "let her dislike one man and approve of another ever so much, it will be expected . . . that she should *deny herself*, when she can *oblige all her family*" (1:298). Clarissa's position is dismissed as "*fancy*," while her parents' determination is "*judgement*." Mrs. Norton also emphasizes that it is Clarissa's "*duty* to comply" and points out that "there would not be any merit in your compliance if it were *not* to be against your own liking" (1:195). She tells Clarissa that while it may "at *present* be disagreeable to you to be thus compelled" in a few months she "very probably" will have great satisfaction from having acted meritoriously. When Clarissa protests—"It is for my *life*"—Mrs. Norton declares, "I consider everything," and offers the doubtful consolation that if she should prove to be unhappy at least it would be by the direction of her parents rather than from following her own will. Implicit in these expositions of what might be termed the parental argument is the sacrifice of the individual to family interests and of happiness to material gain. Furthermore, the deepest feelings of the child are dismissed as "fancy" and attributed to unmaidenly and unworthy sexual attraction.

Despite the social taboos implied by Mrs. Howe's question about a "nice young creature," Richardson makes it clear that sexuality indeed is a factor in Clarissa's aversion to Solmes. She comments sarcastically, "PERSON in a man is nothing, because I am supposed to be prudent: so my eye is to be disgusted . . . and I am to be wedded to a *monster*" (1:79). She describes him as "sitting asquat," a "bent creature" with "splay feet" who resembles nothing so much as "a toad." As Anna Howe comments, "What a dreadful thing must even the *love* of such a husband be!" (1:126), and Clarissa asks, "could it have been honest in me to have given my hand to an odious hand, and to have consented to such a more than reluctant, such an *immiscible* union" with "the marriage intimacies . . . so *very* intimate?" (2:167). Even more important, however, is Solmes's complete lack of intellect or true moral standards. He is described as having "no great capacity," being "coarse and indelicate," "not only narrow but covetous," and lacking both the capacity to enjoy his own wealth and any spirit of charity (1:158). As Clarissa declares, "he wants . . . every qualification that distinguishes a worthy man" (1:287), yet this is the man whom she is asked to pledge to honor and obey. "What a *duration of woe*," she exclaims to Anna, to be bound for life to a "wretch, vested with prerogatives, who will claim rule" although "more ignorant, more illiterate, more low-minded" than his wife who naturally will be tempted to despise him and therefore risk "everyday, it is likely . . . some new breach of an altar-vowed duty" (1:287). In such a marriage Clarissa would not only be committed to a lifetime of misery, but also would compromise her moral integrity. Her adherence to a system of values to which others give only lip service leads her to regard marriage duties as "absolutely indispensable, so solemnly engaged for" (2:167) and, therefore, she reminds her parents, "my *heart* is less concerned in this than my *soul*; my *temporary*, perhaps, than my future good" (1:260).

Her temporal life will be miserable enough, however. Solmes shows unpleasant signs of sadism, observing that "it will be a pleasure to him to see by what pretty little degrees I shall come to" and quoting that "*fear* was a better security than *love,* for a woman's good behaviour" (1:206). Clarissa is well aware that in her world a wife would have almost no recourse. No matter how unhappy her life might be, prudence would dictate submission, because there would be no one "to whom I could appeal with *effect* against a husband," and furthermore the "invincible and avowed dislike I have for him at *setting out,* [would] seem to justify any ill usage from him *in that state*" (1:152). The fact that Solmes persists in his courtship is, as Clarissa points out, sufficient proof of his barbarity. "If you really value me, as my friends would make me believe," she asks him, "must it not be a mean and selfish value? . . . It must be for *your own sake* only, not for *mine*" (1:167). And later she pleads with him, "Do not wish to have a young creature compelled in the most material article of her life, for the sake of motives she despises; and in behalf of a person she cannot value" (1:379).

For Clarissa, the issues are very clear and the solution is simple. Marriage to Solmes is not only unthinkable in terms of worldly happiness, but a real threat to her moral life. The solution is to placate her family in every way possible if she can only obtain the right to refuse Solmes. She will give her estate to Arabella, and, she opines, Solmes has so little delicacy that he will not cavil over which sister he marries. She will also pledge to live single, dependent upon the bounty of her father in return for good behavior, thereby frustrating any hopes Lovelace may have. A plan that appears unexceptionable to her is translated into quite different terms in the ensuing family conference. She is "a vile, artful creature," "a specious hypocrite," scheming to obtain public sympathy by a renunciation that could easily be set aside by Lovelace who, despite her false pledge to remain single, has already declared he is sure of her. They marvel at "the insolence . . . that she who was so justly in disgrace for downright rebellion, should pretend to prescribe to the whole family!—should name a husband for her elder sister!" (1:309). Just as Pamela and the unreformed Mr. B. signified different meanings by the same words because their values were different, so Clarissa's sincere promises seem mere cant to her family, who have abandoned all but nominal Christianity. Both Arabella and James delight in turning moral rhetoric against her, Bella asking how "the *prudent,* nay the *dutiful* and *pi-ous* (so she sneeringly pronounced the word) Clarissa Harlowe should be so strangely fond of a profligate man"

(1:213), while James mocks her "high notion of the matrimonial duty" and advises her to think "a little more of the *filial* duty." They are so caught up in their schemes of power that it is possible to believe that they really cannot understand Clarissa; their own need for self-esteem leads them to see her exemplary life as "ostentation," casting into the shade "all the ladies in the country, who do not do as you do" (1:230). In the face of this, Clarissa finds her world turning into a carnival house of distorting mirrors. Qualities, she tells Anna, "which used so lately to gain me applause, now become my crimes" (1:309–10), and "beloved as I thought myself so lately by every one . . . now I have not one person in the world to plead for me, to stand by me" (1:264).

The pressure mounts as Clarissa is first forbidden to leave the house, then denied access to the parlor, finally becoming a prisoner in her own room where she sometimes is forced to seek refuge in her small writing closet. She is cut off from the outside world, except for her illicit correspondences with Anna and with Lovelace, and even denied access to her own mother and father. A forced marriage is threatened, with the implacable Bella and James in charge. It is reported to Clarissa that "they expect *fits* and *fetches* . . . and expostulations, and exclamations *without number*: but everybody will be prepared for them," and, she is told, "when it's over, it's over; and I shall be easy and pacified when I find I can't help it" (1:462). "Good Dr. Lewen," the Harlowes' pastor and Clarissa's spiritual director, tells her that "he had ever made it a rule, to avoid interfering in the private concerns of families" (1:364). Anna Howe has urged Clarissa to resume her estate as a means of living independently. At one point she reports that "I was so vexed . . . that I took up my pen," intending to follow Anna's advice, "but my heart failed me, when I recollected that I had not one friend to stand by or support me in my claim" (1:264). Her hesitation is undoubtedly prudent—she has already been warned "that there are flaws in her grandfather's will" and that "not a shilling of that estate will be yours if you do not yield" (1:96). Significantly, her family fear litigation over the estate only from Lovelace as husband, not from Clarissa herself.

As the fate of becoming Solmes's wife comes to seem inescapable, Clarissa's only recourse is Lovelace. (Anna Howe is unable to help her friend because of the opposition of her widowed mother whose natural inclination to support parental authority is strengthened by a tentative courtship with Uncle Antony Harlowe.) During this first part of the novel, the reader learns of Lovelace chiefly through the eyes of others. He has a reputation as a libertine, but he also has many redeeming qualities. He is handsome, aristocratic, rich, witty, a good letter writer, a generous landlord, brave, magnanimous in his conduct during the duel with James, and, most importantly, her intellectual equal. Clarissa admits that she has difficulty in keeping up the dislike she considers that she should feel because of his failings when she considers his many good qualities, adding, "And then has the secret pleasure intruded itself, to be able to reclaim such a man to the paths of virtue and honour" (1:200). As her family's tyranny makes a forced marriage with the odious Solmes seem a real possibility, escape with Lovelace inevitably appears preferable. "How, my dear," Clarissa writes to Anna, "am I driven on one side, and invited on the other!" (1:409). Richardson shapes his narrative so that the reader, like Anna Howe, also evaluates the alternatives in Lovelace's favor. Through Clarissa's reports, often direct transcriptions of conversations, we are acutely aware of the mean-spirited intransigence of the Harlowes; Lovelace, on the other hand, is a far less vivid figure. Before Clarissa's "elopement" only three of ninety-two letters are written by Lovelace. His messages to Clarissa herself are reported at secondhand, and they are generally encouraging promises of love and respect, coupled with vows to abide by her decisions in regard to his own hopes if only he can prevent marriage to Solmes. The reader, through Lovelace's own revelations to his friend Belford, learns more about him than Clarissa does, but despite Richardson's declaration that "in the very first Letter of Lovelace all those Seeds of Wickedness were thick sown, which sprouted up into Action afterwards in his Character,"[7] we are more apt to be engaged by his energy, disarmed by his acknowledgment of his own faults, and encouraged by his suggestions that he may now be ready to reform, since he asserts, "I cannot say that I was ever in love before. . . . But now am I *indeed* in love" (1:145-46).

After Clarissa is tricked into running away, the balance of the letters shifts, giving a much clearer picture of Lovelace through his own words. His chief correspondent is "Jack" Belford, a fellow libertine, to whom he reveals all his schemes in a spirit of vaunting rakish camaraderie. Belford gradually becomes an advocate for Clarissa, and, like Anna Howe, serves to provoke self-revelation by probing his friend's motives. The unfolding of Lovelace's true nature is of dominant importance in this part of the novel as it becomes increasingly evident that Clarissa's chance for worldly happiness is dependent upon him. Richardson has taken the stock figure of the Restoration rake, often depicted as a vigorous, individualistic, rather sympathetic antihero in the world of comedy, and shown the ultimate sterility of his code, its destructiveness not merely to his victims, but to the rake himself. In this first letter Lovelace does, in fact, reveal the key to his character. Quoting Dryden, he boasts that his is not a "gentle nature" in which love may inspire a "gentle fire," but rather one of those "tempestuous souls" whom "raging flames . . . invade" as "with Pride it mounts, and with Revenge it glows" (1:147). In the same letter that suggests the possibility of true love bringing about his reformation, he also glories in the thought of securing Clarissa "in spite of them all; in spite of her own inflexible heart: mine, without condition; without reformation," and thereby having her whole family "come creeping to me . . . to kneel at the footstool of my throne" (1:148). Furthermore, since Clarissa is an exemplar, a model woman, "to carry off such a girl as this, . . . what a triumph! What a triumph over the whole sex!" (1:150). He concludes his letter, declaring that he is focused "upon REVENGE, which I love; upon LOVE which I hate, *heartily* hate, because 'tis my master" (1:152).

Clarissa is now engaged in a new power struggle in which she is once again merely a token—on the one hand in a masculine duel for supremacy between Lovelace and her family whom he hates for their rejection of his suit, and on the other hand, even more dangerously, in Lovelace's own psychomachy. Dominating Lovelace's view of women are two contradictory images. In one, they are the weaker sex, inherently corrupt, and kept from indulging their true natures only by the artificial and hypocritical code society imposes upon them. Lovelace is fond of quoting Pope's line, "Every woman is at heart a rake." While decorum demands that a woman say no, women secretly admire libertines rather than tame suitors because they want to be forced. "What woman answers *affirmatively* to the question?" Lovelace asks, and believes that "*once subdued, is always subdued*" (2:363). He explains to Belford, "there may be *consent in struggle*; there may be *yielding in resistance,*" and the point to be tried is whether such conflict "may not be weaker and weaker, till the *willingness* ensue" (2:245). In contradiction to this, Lovelace hopes to find a truly virtuous woman since only such a woman is worthy of being his wife. "Libertines are nicer," he explains, "than other men" because they judge women "by the frailty of those they have triumphed over" (2:35). As to Clarissa, "It was her character that drew me to her; and it was her beauty and good sense that riveted my chains" (2:38), but, he continues, "What must be that virtue which will not stand a trial?" (2:40), and "if she resist—if she nobly stand her trial? Why then will I marry her, and bless my stars for such an angel" (2:41). Marriage, in Lovelace's eyes, fully compensates for every indignity.

Blended with this dualistic view of women is Lovelace's overriding egotism and a broad streak of sadism. He glories in his ability to control others through his stratagems. "I love when I dig a pit," he declares, "to have my prey tumble in with secure feet and open eyes"; then, he continues, "a man can look down upon her, with an *O-ho charmer, how came you there?*" (2:102). For him, he explains, the chase is all. "*Preparation* and *expectation* are in a manner everything," especially for a man characterized by "A love of intrigue. An invention for mischief. A triumph in subduing," while "the fruition, what is there in that?" (1:173). He declares, "I am no sensual man; but a man of spirit," one who has "ever had more pleasure in my contrivances than in the end of them" (2:147). His fantasies all picture Clarissa humbled, in tears, suing for his favor. "I am half-sorry to say," he writes, "*that I find a pleasure in playing the tyrant over what I love*" (3:65). He justifies his pleasure in cruelty by declaring of women, "that sex is made to bear pain . . . and they love those best, whether man or child, who give them most" (3:450–51). Clarissa has been quite correct when she judges him to be "*a hard-hearted man*" and confides to Anna, "*I have thought more than once, that he had rather see me in tears than give me reason to be pleased with him*" (2:465).

For Lovelace, as for her family, Clarissa is not really an individual at all. In fact, their attitudes are remarkably similar. For both, assertion of the will is paramount. As we have seen, Clarissa's father is determined that he "will not be baffled by her," while Lovelace speaks of "the contention that her vigilance has set on foot, *which* shall overcome the *other*" (2:142), and declares that the struggle is only "whether I am to have her in *my own way,* or in *hers*" (3:92). Just as Clarissa's family disregard any sexual preference she may have, seeing her revulsion at Solmes or her attraction to Lovelace as mere "fancy," so Lovelace also discounts any particularity in sexual satisfaction. "The most charming woman on earth, were she an empress, can excel the meanest in the customary visibles only" (2:142), he declares, assuring the servant, Joseph Leman, "one woman is like another" (2:147). In fact, he finds little satisfaction in the sexual act, "for that's a vapour, a bubble" (2:337). Just as the Harlowes' choices are restricted by their fear of the world's opinion, so Lovelace is worried about "what a figure should I make in rakish annals" were he to marry with "the lady in my power"

(2:250). And for both, women assume value only when connected to men. Lovelace asserts the accepted double standard of the rake, boasting, "*I never lied to man and hardly ever said truth to woman*" (4:445). Belford notes that rakes "consider all those of the sex as fair prize" (2:158), although he also declares that "adultery is so capital a guilt, that even rakes and libertines . . . disavow and condemn it" (2:332). The point here, of course, is that adultery harms a man by tampering with his property. The rake's code echoes James Harlowe's confident assumption that Clarissa's destiny is to serve his masculine ego.

Lovelace is confident that he, experienced in the techniques of seduction and now in control of Clarissa's living arrangements, will succeed in seducing her. He plans to "watch her every step to find one sliding one; her every moment to find the critical one," knowing that his advances come from "a man she hated not" (2:42). Like the Harlowes, Lovelace underestimates Clarissa. Her family had counted on the continuation of her former conduct as a docile and obedient daughter. Anna Howe regretfully predicted that "they will subdue such a fine spirit as yours, unused to opposition" and ironically noted that "the world . . . [will] admire you for your blind duty and will-less resignation" (1:67). Clarissa knows that her family "have all an absolute dependence upon what they suppose to be a meekness in my temper" but, she asserts, "I verily think . . . that I have almost as much in me of my father's as of my mother's family" (1:37). For Clarissa, the chief point is moral: "I never *ought* to be Mrs. Solmes. I repeat that I *ought* not" (1:93), and she asks, "is not my sincerity, is not the integrity of my heart, concerned in my answer?" (1:103). Such a marriage will endanger, if not destroy, her moral life. Clarissa, however, like Pamela, also has her own share of human pride that aids her first in her struggle with her brother, and later with Lovelace. "What right have *you* to dispose of my hand?," she indignantly asks James, declaring "if you govern everybody else, you shall not govern me" (1:381). So, later she says of Lovelace, "If I must be humbled, it had better be by those to whom I owe duty, than by him" (2:265), and warns him, "I confess that I have as much *pride* as you can have" (2:300).

More important, however, is what Clarissa calls "steadiness." "*Steadiness of mind* (a quality which the ill-bred and censorious deny to any of our sex) when we are absolutely convinced of being in the right . . . brings great credit to the possessor of it" (1:93). Her mother's example of submissive obedience has taught her the futility of seeking peace through forbearance, demonstrating only that "those who will bear much have much to bear" (1:93). For Clarissa, "to be *self-acquitted* is a blessing to be preferred to the opinion of all the world" (1:458), and she hopes that "we may make the world allow for and respect us as we please, if we can be sturdy in our wills, and set out accordingly. It is but being the *less* beloved for it, that's all" (1:22–23). She is perhaps overly optimistic about her fate during her lifetime, but her reliance on her own moral perception, a perception that grows and strengthens during her ordeal, enables her to thwart Lovelace's never-ending stratagems. He has declared that she will merit "honours next to divine" if she can give proof "that there was once a woman whose virtue no trials, no stratagems, no temptations, even from a man she hated not, could overpower" (2:42). This is exactly what Clarissa does.

During their extended duel, Clarissa varies somewhat in her attitude toward Lovelace. This is only natural, first, because he is indeed a master of artifice and disguise, "a perfect Proteus," as Clarissa says, and, second, because Lovelace himself wavers, at times sincerely intending to marry and reform. The first instances create moments where dramatic irony heightens the pathos of Clarissa's position. Before leaving the Harlowe house, Clarissa has confessed, "I like him better than ever I thought I should like him; . . . better perhaps than I *ought* to like him" (1:203), and we see that she could indeed love Lovelace if he would act with ordinary decency. On one occasion she writes to Anna, "I cannot but call this, my circumstances considered, a happy day to the end of it," confessing, "Indeed my dear, I think I could prefer him to all the men I ever knew, were he to be always what he has been this day" (2:225). From Lovelace's letters the reader knows, and regrets, that actually he is merely trying to ingratiate himself in furtherance of a plot to invade her bedchamber. At other times, however, Lovelace is sincere in his protestations, if only momentarily. When Belford chides that it is impossible that he should break oaths and protestations so solemn, Lovelace replies, "That I did *not* intend it is certain," characteristically then adding, "But knowest thou not my aversion to the state of shackles? And is she not IN MY POWER?" (1:514). The reader experiences this vacillation again and again. Even shortly before the actual rape, Lovelace, touched by her distress, reports, "I forgot at the instant all my vows of revenge," he tearfully pleads for her pardon, "honourably and justly" (3:141). Later that night, however, he again reflects, "what a figure shall I make in rakish annals? And can I have taken all these pains for nothing?" The reader learns what Clarissa has already suspected, that Lovelace "wants a *heart*" (1:202); his obsession with domination and power have made a normal loving relationship impossible. A sense of waste pervades our perception of Lovelace's childish schemes. For him, Clarissa is just the supreme quarry, providing "a field for stratagem and contrivance" and holding out the possibility of "a triumph over the whole sex! And then such a revenge to gratify" (1:150). In contrast, Clarissa, looking back, says, "Poor man," admitting, "I once could have loved him. . . . I think I could have made him happy" (4:306). Anna Howe, early in the novel, has told Clarissa ironically, "You are all too rich to be happy, child," explaining that her family is obsessed with becoming "*still* richer" so that "true happiness" is no longer "any part of your family view" (1:41). Lovelace has also cut himself off from any chance of true happiness by his blind pursuit of "the joys of the chase . . . the joys that fill the mind of the inventive or contriving genius" (2:30). At first Lovelace has seemed more attractive than the Harlowes because his goal is "love," "the divine Clarissa," rather than sordid gain. In the second part of the novel we learn that there is little difference between them. Both are egoists willing to be cruel to gain power. Both see Clarissa not as an individual with her own rights and needs but as a playing piece in their games of dominance. Both are so caught up in a world of distorted values that faith in their own fictions makes it virtually impossible for them to understand Clarissa's world founded upon a belief in truth as a principle of behavior and in the sacred importance of each individual's soul.

Lovelace's male pride will not permit him to admit defeat. Even in the rake's code there are certain acknowledged limits. Belford warns Lovelace against any use of "*unmanly artifices*" (2:254). And Lovelace himself has said, "Abhorred be *force*. . . . There is no triumph in *force*. No conquest over the will" (2:398). Finally, however, he drugs Clarissa and rapes her in the desperate hope that having been "*once overcome, she will be always overcome*" (2:398). Just as the Harlowes expected that while there may be "*fits* and *fetches*" at first, "when it's over, it's over" and she will then be "easy and pacified," so Lovelace is confident that "the haughty beauty will not refuse me, when her pride of being corporally inviolate is brought down" (3:190). He indulges in one of his fantasies of domination in which Clarissa is seen with "her face averted: speech lost in sighs—abashed—conscious—" while he is triumphant, gazing at "her downcast countenance!" (3:218).

The reality is quite different. In their first meeting after the rape, it is Lovelace who is abashed, Clarissa who is dignified and composed. "Whose the triumph now!" he exclaims, "HERS or MINE?" (3:221). The final third of the book describes Clarissa coming to terms with her experience and preparing for a Christian death, while Lovelace continues his futile vacillations between rakish pride and his attraction to Clarissa. In her temporary derangement resulting, we are told, chiefly from the opiates used, Clarissa writes a number of fragments, later found in her room and preserved by Lovelace. These messages from her subconscious show important perspectives on her experience that will later be clarified by Clarissa's fully rational statements. First, there is the question of her own responsibility for the rape. Paper 3 tells the fable of a young lady who raised a wild animal—lion, bear or tiger— from a cub, priding herself on its tameness, until, "neglecting to satisfy its hungry maw, or having otherwise disobliged it on some occasion, it resumed its nature; and on a sudden fell upon her, and tore her in pieces" (3:206). The fragment concludes by asking who was most to blame, and answering, "The lady, surely! For what *she* did was *out* of nature, *out* of character, at least: what it did was *in* its own nature." Later, Clarissa will declare to Belford that although "there were some hard circumstances in her case . . . not *one* person, throughout the whole fatal transaction, had acted out of character, but *herself* " (3:500). Clarissa has always made it clear that "to be *self-acquitted* is a blessing to be preferred to the opinion of all the world" (1:458), and therefore her own judgment of her behavior is of the greatest importance.

Several fragments refer to her pride. "How art thou now humbled in the dust, thou proud Clarissa Harlowe!," paper 4 begins, reflecting on the past when she would "go to rest satisfied with the adulations paid" and concluding that she could put off all temptations but that of "vanity" (3:206). Paper 5, addressed to her sister, declares that Bella was correct in judging her to be proud: "You knew me better than I knew myself"; and confesses, "I was too secure in the knowledge I thought I had of my own heart" (3:207). Paper 6 continues the theme, regretting that there is "No court now to be paid to my smiles" (3:207). Increasingly, after her escape with Lovelace, Clarissa has been forced to question the purity of her own motives, and to conclude that she is indeed tainted by the first of the capital sins. She reflects that not only did she take pride "in the applause of everyone," but even "in supposing I had *not* that pride," concealed as it was from her "unexamining heart under the specious veil of *humility*" (2:378). Lovelace has sarcastically analyzed Clarissa's attraction to him, a known rake, as a desire "to have the merit of reclaiming him," deriding her "pretty notions [of] how charmingly it would look to have a penitent of her own making dangling at her side to church, through an applauding neighborhood" (3:316), and Clarissa admits to his aunt, Lady Betty, that she did "hope that I might be an humble means in the hand of Providence" to reclaim him, a motive she now regards as "punishably presumptuous" (3:335).

The fragments also acknowledge her attraction to Lovelace. The young lady of paper 3 "took a great fancy" to the young cub, and paper 8 states explicitly, "At first, I saw something in your air and person that displeased me not" (3:208), explaining that he seemed brave and generous, and that "thus prepossessed" she found "whatever qualities I *wished* to find." Clarissa has previously acknowledged that *"If I had never valued him, he would never have had it in his power to insult me"* (3:137), and she later writes to Mrs. Norton, *"I once could have loved him. . . . Yet he never deserved my love"* (3:345). In the first part of the novel, Anna Howe rallies her friend about falling in love, while Clarissa denies the imputed "throbs," but now she does come to terms with her own sexuality and admits that not only did she love Lovelace, but "vainly believed that he loved me" (3:520).

The papers speak most poignantly, however, of waste, of the irretrievable loss of potential human happiness and fulfillment. Paper 6 asks, "What now is become of the prospects of a happy life, which once I thought opening before me?" (2:207), describing an idealized vision of the virtuous bride preparing for marriage. The vision embodies a good portion of that pride that Clarissa has already admitted, with its "encouraging compliments," and "elevation . . . for conscious merit." It is, in fact, a typical adolescent dream of the bridal day with its "solemn preparations" and "nuptial ornaments," with a "prostrate adorer," "an admiring world," and "rejoicing parents and relatives." This is not the saintlike, otherworldly, Clarissa whom we will eventually admire, but it does suggest a normal young woman's fantasy of her "great day," the one day on which she is the acknowledged center of attention, surrounded by love and admiration. It makes us aware of the normal, everyday pleasures of which Clarissa, who is, after all, only nineteen, has been so needlessly deprived. Paper 7 amplifies the theme, addressing the "pernicious caterpillar, that preyest upon the fair leaf of virgin fame, and poisonest those leaves which thou canst not devour!" (3:207). As Mark Kinkead-Weekes has suggested, the dominant emphasis in this fragment is not so much "violation or desecration of purity, but upon the destruction of potential fertility, growth, warmth and colour."[8] The "eating cankerworm" preys upon "the opening bud, and turnest the damask rose into livid yellowness!" The "fell blight" destroys "the early promises of the shining year!" That which should grow and develop into full beauty, into nourishing fulfillment, is wastefully spoiled. The passage shows Clarissa's view of sexuality to be sharply different from that of Lovelace. She sees it as potentiality for growth that with the care of the "husbandman" will yield a bountiful harvest of mutual love and understanding; Lovelace, as we have seen, views it as egoistic conquest. The fragment laments the blasting of "joyful hopes" and reminds Lovelace that God judges "by our benevolent or evil actions to one another."

Paper 9 makes clear how deeply she now despises Lovelace. She writes, "Had the happiness of the poorest outcast in the world, whom I had never seen, never known, never before heard of, lain as much in *my* power as my happiness did in *yours,*" that her heart would have made her fly to the rescue. Any human being, no matter how lowly or remote, should make demands upon our humanity. Lovelace, in contrast, has been unable, like the Harlowes and Solmes, to recognize her rights as an individual. The rape is not merely a physical violation but an attempt to destroy her psyche, a violation of the essential core of her being. This is what Lovelace means by "once subdued, always subdued," and this is why he is driven to actions unacceptable even by the code of the libertine. Clarissa, while acknowledging her own pride and her attraction to Lovelace, shows, even in these fragments, that she can progress from self-accusation to a clearer view. "Yet, God knows my heart," she writes in paper 8, "I had no culpable inclinations!" (3:208). She can truthfully declare that she honored virtue and hated vice. Her mistake was in not recognizing that Lovelace was "vice itself," a natural failure because she "judged of [other's] hearts by my own." This is perhaps a lack of worldly wisdom, but certainly not a capital error.

The last fragment, paper 10, is a collection of quotations from various authors—Shakespeare, Dryden, Cowley, and others—that suggests the difficulty Clarissa has in coming to terms with evil. The quotations, by allusion to such works as *Hamlet* or Cowley's *Despair,* suggest that contending with the presence, indeed with the prosperity, of evil in a world believed to be governed by a beneficent God is a problem that has taxed poets and philosophers through the ages. The passage ends with lines from Dryden's *Absalom and Achitophel*: "For Life can never be sincerely blest, / Heav'n punishes the *Bad,* and proves the *Best."* This is the traditional Christian answer—the ways of God are unsearchable, human understanding is limited, earthly life is a time of trial, but the good are assured of their reward in eternity. Clarissa has maintained her "steadiness," her firmness of moral vision, in the face of persecution from both her family and from Lovelace. She now emerges from the rape—an experience designed to shatter and humiliate her—with a spiritual purpose that has been strengthened and clarified. She accepts the mystery at the heart of her faith and renews her belief in the essential goodness of God. The last part of the book, which modern readers tend to find dull and anticlimactic, is necessary to prove Clarissa a true exemplar. A parallel can be made to the last third of the original *Pamela*, which modern readers also find tedious, but which establishes Pamela as truly virtuous.

After the rape Clarissa never thinks of Lovelace as a possible husband. Once again she shows her difference from even such well meaning, "good" people as Anna Howe and Mrs. Howe, her cousin Morden, or Lovelace's relatives. For Clarissa, the issue is simple. If she could not marry Solmes because she could not promise to love, honor, and obey him, how, then, could she possibly marry Lovelace? She states, "I was not *capable* of resolving to give my *hand,* and—*nothing but my hand,*" asking "Have I not given a flagrant proof of this to the once most indulgent of parents?" (3:117). How, then, could she "submit to make that man my choice, whose actions are, and ought to be, my abhorrence!" (3:519). She tells her cousin Morden that she can indeed forgive Lovelace, because she feels superior to him. "Can I be above the man, sir, to whom I shall give my hand and vows?" she asks, and can she, by marriage, give "a sanction to the most premeditated baseness?" (4:250). Her friends all urge marriage as the only possible way of salvaging her reputation and as a prerequisite to reconciliation with her family. Lovelace's relatives plead with her to give him this chance for reparation. Clarissa finds it incredible that Anna could think her "so lost, so *sunk* at least, as that she could for the sake of patching up, in the world's eye, a broken reputation" be brought to "vow duty to one so wicked" (3:519–20).

Lovelace has committed the rape, a desperate action that contravenes even his own rakish code, because he is confident that it will change Clarissa, that she will afterward lose self-esteem, be humbled, and turn to him as her only possible savior. He also hopes, although her drugged state makes this rather improbable, that she will now become "true woman," that is, aware of her own sensual nature and therefore subject to "the god of love." He fantasizes, for example, that she may be pregnant, and will give birth to twin boys, thereby becoming still more dependent on his generosity for legitimizing her offspring and also, of course, demonstrating that she is completely human, not angelic. The rape does indeed change Clarissa—it forces her to see that by hoping for "either morality, gratitude, or humanity, from a libertine" she was ignoring the fact that "to *be* a libertine" he "must have got over and defied all moral sanctions" (3:221). Her deepest regret, she tells Lovelace, is that "I saw thee not sooner in thy proper colours." While Lovelace hopes that the rape will force Clarissa to abandon what he sees as merely a conventional facade of morality, it returns her irrevocably to her first principles, demonstrating that morality in its fullest sense is the essential core of her being. Clarissa has been deeply attracted by Lovelace. Anna Howe, early in the novel, is the first to recognize this and, when Clarissa protests that she refuses to be "*in love* with him" because of his faulty morals, ironically congratulates her friend "on your being the first of our sex that ever I heard of who has been able to turn that lion, Love, at her own pleasure, into a lap-dog" (1:49). Clarissa's paper after the rape about the lady and the lion cub shows that she has recognized her own presumption in believing herself capable of "taming" Lovelace and of ignoring her own sexuality, but in a more important sense, Anna's ironic comment has been correct. Clarissa's victory over Lovelace is a vindication of her "steadiness," of her clear moral vision. Belford sums up the way Clarissa's actions appear to him. "How worthy of herself," he says, "that it [the rape] has made her *hate* the man she once *loved*!," continuing, "And rather than marry him, choose to expose her disgrace to the whole world; to forego the reconciliation with her friends which her heart was so set upon; and to hazard a thousand evils to which her youth and her sex may too probably expose an indigent and friendless beauty" (3:314). He sees her rejection of marriage as a heroic sacrifice of all that society holds dear— reputation, security, wealth, friendship. It is the mark of Clarissa's moral integrity, however, that she sees herself simply as following the only possible course. Once she knows Lovelace's true character, she can only despise him.

Clear-sightedly, she also recognizes that "I have had an escape, rather than a loss, in missing Mr. Lovelace for a husband," explaining that, considering "the *cruelty of his nature,* and the *sportiveness of his invention,* together with the *high opinion he has of himself,* it will not be doubted that a wife of his must have been miserable; and more miserable if she loved him" (4:58). Lovelace amply demonstrates that this judgment is correct by his vacillations and grotesque fantasies, even when he is declaring himself overwhelmed with remorse. For example, he exclaims in despair, "Oh return, return, thou only charmer of my soul!," declaring that he now knows "the value of the jewel he has slighted" (3:388), but a few days later, chafing at the idea of wedlock, comforts himself with the notion of dalliance with Anna Howe, noting that "if a man's wife has a dear friend of her sex, a hundred liberties may be taken with that friend" (3:412).

Clarissa not only rejects marriage to Lovelace as morally impossible, she now has very little interest in the everyday, respectable world that has revealed its spiritual emptiness so persistently. The question, "Why does Clarissa die?" is probably, like "How many children had Lady Macbeth?," a question that should not be asked. The best answer is because it is artistically necessary.[9] Richardson himself, in the post-script to *Clarissa* declared that "Heaven *only* could reward" (4:558) his heroine. In terms of verisimilitude no eighteenth-century reader would wonder that Clarissa's ordeals, including, after the rape, her false imprisonment for debt, would cause her health to falter. The relation between mental and physical health was a cornerstone of medical treatment in the century. Richardson himself, describing his poor health to Lady Bradshaigh, attributed it to a series of "repeated Blows,"[10] sorrows caused by the deaths of friends and relatives. In the last portion of the book we see Clarissa becoming more and more indifferent to a world that has come to seem alien and unimportant. Our knowledge of her last days comes from Belford, the reformed rake. He is protective and admiring, but just as Clarissa inevitably was misunderstood by the Harlowes and by Lovelace, now she is misunderstood even by the good people who surround her. Her preparations for death, including the purchase of a coffin, are not morbid, as they see them, but practical. In the same spirit, she drapes a cloth over the coffin and makes it useful in her cramped quarters as a writing table. The true Christian should always feel that heaven is preferable to earthly travail, and the last year of Clarissa's life has shown her a brutal world of greed, aggression, and pathological egoism. Why should she not prefer the joys of eternity? Clarissa's pride is never wholly conquered, and she realizes that, even if she could regain her estate and live the useful single life she once coveted, it would be tainted. She would always be an object of pity and speculation as to "why Clarissa Harlowe chose solitude" (3:521), and her ability to do good would be hindered. More importantly, however, Clarissa now has truly gained the end sought by most systems of spiritual exercises—indifference to worldly desires. Even the continued implacable coldness of her family loses its capacity for hurt, and, near death, Clarissa can assert, "GOD ALMIGHTY WOULD NOT LET ME DEPEND FOR COMFORT UPON ANY BUT HIMSELF" (4:339). She dies at peace with herself and with her God.

The long, slow modulation of Clarissa toward perfect serenity is contrasted with the agitated posturings of Lovelace and with the grotesque deathbed of "Mother" Sinclair, the keeper of the house of prostitution where Clarissa is raped. This is a moralistic set-piece, with the prostitutes revealing their physical decay in the clear light of day, gathered round the "old wretch" who is "raving, crying, cursing, and even howling, more like a wolf than a human creature" (4:380). She refuses to take moral responsibility for her own actions, thrusting the blame on others, and reveals her continued attachment to worldly values by, in effect, trying to bribe God, offering to leave all her money to charity if she can be granted a little more of life. The contrast between a Christian death and the agonized torments of the wicked is abundantly clear. The more exemplary contrast, however, is between the use that Clarissa makes of her experience in contrast to Lovelace.

As we have seen, both Clarissa and Lovelace stand outside of the world of normal social values. Clarissa at first does not realize that this is true. Believing that her society does embody the morality that it professes, she lives happily within it and anticipates an equally happy future. She has confidence in her own abilities, intelligence, and judgment that have always proved more than adequate, and while she recognizes that life will always present some trials, she confronts the world with the assurance of a cherished, talented nineteen year old. In the conflict with her family she learns that the beneficent love she took for granted is no match for overweening venality, and that their Christian principles are a hypocritical facade to conceal brutal selfishness. Striving to preserve her moral integrity, she takes what seems the only alternative course and flies with Lovelace. In the conflict with Lovelace she learns that her judgment has been misled, and that she has seen his character in terms of her hopes rather than reality. His conduct demonstrates that she has been ready to love a man who never deserved that love. From this disillusionment with all she has valued so highly, not only her love for her family and her attraction to Lovelace but her satisfaction with her own conduct, she wins through to a new sense of

personal integrity and transcendent morality. She is at last truly herself
in the way granted to the great saints who have conquered not only
the world but the dark night of the soul.

In contrast, Lovelace does not change at all. The shallow egoism
that is the foundation of his rebellion against accepted values prevents
him from making any use of his experiences. The true libertine, often
presented as a rather attractive figure who flouts hypocritical decorum
in the cause of "nature," is shown to be the most unnatural of beings.
Lovelace's name would have been pronounced "loveless," and we see
that he is indeed trapped in a code that adulates power and denigrates
love, even love in the limited sense of sexual enjoyment. Lovelace declares that "the crowning act" of seduction is "a vapour, a bubble!"
(2:337), and his bizarre fantasies of debauching the decorous widow
who shelters Clarissa in Hampstead, or raping Anna's mother, demonstrate what modern psychology acknowledges—the rapist is motivated not by sexual attraction but by hatred. Lovelace's fate is much
more pathetic than Clarissa's because it represents a total waste of human potentiality. There are times when he wavers and seems capable
of breaking out of his solipsistic prison, but fear of looking foolish in
"rakish annals" deters him. In fact, we come to realize, Lovelace is
incapable both of an adult sexual relationship and of any truly loving
relationship. His supreme value is triumph; he conceives of other human beings only in terms of victory and defeat. His energy, his intelligence, his humor, all his attractive qualities, become agents of
destruction. He learns nothing, retreating into self-pity, and blaming
Sinclair and her whores for his deed. He dies in a duel with Clarissa's
cousin Morden, a duel he, characteristically, is sure he will win. His
servant reports him as "very unwilling to die" and, in a final flight of
egotism, he exclaims, "LET THIS EXPIATE!" as he expires.

While Clarissa's death assures us of her eternal happiness, we do,
together with Anna and her now repentant family, feel great waste here
also. Clarissa clearly would have brought happiness to many and en-
riched the possibilities of her world if she had lived. While Lovelace
and through him the double standard of the libertine are expressly
condemned, Richardson reminds his reader of the responsibility "respectable" society bears in the fate of Clarissa. As we have seen, Clarissa
could find no ally in her struggle with her family. The "good Dr.
Lewen," her minister, refuses to intervene, and Anna, her friend, is
helpless because of the same disabilities of parental control and the
dependent position of women that frustrate Clarissa. In her contest

with Lovelace it is clear that a male, especially one with any claim to privilege and rank, will find it easy to defeat a woman, even if she has claims to position and virtue. Two incidents will serve as illustration: Lovelace's success in Hampstead and his reception, later, at a neighborhood ball. One night at Sinclair's house, Lovelace has staged a fire as a pretext to gain access to Clarissa in her bedchamber. Disgusted by his stratagems and by his freedoms, she resolves to escape and succeeds in getting to Hampstead, where she takes lodgings at a Mrs. Moore's while awaiting news from Anna Howe about further schemes of flight. Lovelace quickly traces her to Hampstead, and as quickly wins over Mrs. Moore and her women friends. Clarissa has thought the women to be her allies, and laments, "What defence have I against a man, who, go where I will, can turn every one, even of the virtuous of my sex, in his favour?" (3:77). Lovelace successfully imposes himself as a wronged husband and Clarissa as an overdelicate, cold bride. Despite the fact that the women suspect he is, or has been, "a wild fellow," their sympathies go to him and they become his accomplices. One, the widow Bevis, even consents to disguising herself as Clarissa in order to intercept a crucial letter from Anna. Even more shocking is the reception of Lovelace, after the rape, by a group of gentry from Clarissa's neighborhood. Although they know that she has been vilely treated by Lovelace, Anna Howe is the only person at the ball who openly shows her displeasure. The extent to which society will condone the rake is shown by the flirtatious behavior of the women and the careful respect of the men. Anna is furious to see "how pleased half the giddy fools of our sex were with him, notwithstanding his notorious wicked character" (4:23).

Anna and, later, Dr. Lewen urge Clarissa to prosecute Lovelace, in justice not only to herself but to women in general. Clarissa agrees that as a rapist Lovelace should be brought to justice, but she has great doubts as to the efficacy of legal proceedings. Her evidence would be "bandied about, and jested profligately with" and she "would have . . . a ready retort from *every* mouth, that I ought not to have thrown myself into the power of such a man, and that I ought to take for my pains what had befallen me" (4:184–85). From what we have seen of the ready acceptance of Lovelace by those who should be Clarissa's supporters we are forced to agree that she is most probably correct. Furthermore, she notes, even if he should be condemned, "can it be thought that his family would not have had interest enough to obtain pardon for a crime thought too lightly of," and especially when he

"offered me early all the reparation in his power to make?" (4:185).
Society is in accord with the libertine's notion that marriage atones for
all indignities. Just as Clarissa was undoubtedly correct in her judgment that litigation to obtain her estate from her father would have
small chance for success, so is she clear-sighted in her estimate of the
usefulness of legal proceedings against Lovelace. The law was written,
interpreted, and executed by men who would, quite naturally, themselves be imbued with the patriarchal and libertine assumptions of
their society. Clarissa, even though she is a woman of some wealth and
social standing, has no realistic legal recourse available to her in her
struggle.

The most fully developed of the secondary characters in the novel is
Anna Howe. Belford, Lovelace's chief correspondent, serves an important structural purpose in the novel as a vehicle for giving us insight
into Lovelace's most private thoughts and as the final collector and
arranger of the letters. Belford is, however, a somewhat flat character.
Lovelace characterizes him as "a sober dog," twitting him with lacking
inventiveness and spirit. While the reader learns to question the value
of Lovelace's own ingenuity Belford does seem rather passive, and even
Lovelace taunts him with the fact that although he knew Lovelace's
plans and sympathized with Clarissa, he did nothing to rescue her.
Belford remains a narrative convenience.

Anna Howe, while fulfilling structural functions, also becomes a
rounded, interesting personage. As we have seen, she is the confidant
to whom Clarissa entrusts her inmost thoughts with perfect frankness.
Like Belford, Anna provides a contrast to her friend. As Anna puts it,
"I am fitter for *this* world than you; you for the *next* than me—that's
the difference" (1:43). Anna's sharp tongue and witty perceptions provide harsher pictures of the Harlowes than would be suitable from or
characteristic of the loving Clarissa. Anna's good sense and fundamen-
tally sound moral judgment (when she knows the full truth she agrees
that Clarissa should not marry Lovelace) are an important resource for
her friend in her lonely ordeal. Lovelace recognizes the danger that
Anna poses and tries to intercept her letters, succeeding at a crucial
juncture when Anna warns Clarissa of the true nature of Sinclair's
house. In addition to her role as foil and catalyst, however, Anna comes
to be an additional example of the difficulties confronting an intelligent, high spirited woman within the century's accepted code of courtship and marriage. Clarissa's ordeal, while perfectly plausible, could
not be considered typical. Thankfully, most parents were not as in-

transigent and grasping as the Harlowes; almost certainly, few rakes were as resourceful and intrepid as Lovelace. Anna's courtship by Hickman, however, seems not merely plausible but all too probable and exemplifies a dilemma facing many women, given the mores of the period.

Marriage was seen as the natural and desirable state for women, ordained by God and honored by man. In fact, there was no other acceptable role open to women. Spinsters were objects of pity or derision who had no useful role to play in a society in which the extended family was fast becoming an anachronism. As Ian Watt has pointed out, the pejorative meaning of spinster as "old maid" enters the language, according to the *O.E.D.,* in 1719.[11] Single women had lost their useful status in the household and there were no careers open to them except the drudgery of the infant school teacher, the laundress, the housemaid, the seamstress, or, considered the most desirable, the governess or lady's companion. All higher education was closed to women, automatically debarring them from the professions. While lower-class women might keep shops, such an occupation was not genteel and was usually restricted, in fact, to wives, daughters, or widows of merchants. Clarissa maintains that she prefers the single life and is willing to renounce marriage; her society would have seen this declaration as foolishly extreme, and her family simply do not believe her. Joined to the universal denigration of the single state for women was the absolutism of the codes of wedlock, prescribed by sacramental oath and enforced by civil law. A wife had no legal existence, as we have seen in chapter 2; her property and her person were controlled absolutely by her husband. She not only promised to love, honor, and obey her husband, but extremists, such as the Reverend John Sprint, who preached a famous wedding sermon, held it sinful for a wife to question her husband's conduct even in her inmost thoughts. Clarissa realizes that marriage to the odious Solmes could not help but provoke daily breaches of "an altar-vowed duty," but such a high standard presented serious problems to any pious but intelligent woman.

Anna Howe is well aware of these problems. Her suitor, Mr. Hickman, is a worthy but dull young man who is clearly no match for Anna's playful vivacity and keen intelligence. Her mother is anxious to have Anna "married off" to so suitable a candidate, and to her credit his good moral behavior is her principle concern. Anna acknowledges Hickman's merits, but longs for something better. At one point, writing to Clarissa, she depicts, in an amusingly satirical vein, Solmes,

Lovelace, and Hickman as boys, commenting, "that you and I should have such baboons as these to choose out of, is a mortifying thing, my dear" (1:244). While parents ideally gave daughters the right of refusing suitors they disliked, it was also true that the woman's role in courtship was entirely passive. They could not seek a suitable match, as, for example, Lovelace sought out Clarissa. Family and friends, could, of course, put out feelers through various contacts, and encourage an offer as, for example, the Harlowes encouraged Solmes, but possibilities remained limited for most women, especially when families generally expected parity of fortune as a prerequisite. The talented woman could find herself in the uncomfortable position of becoming a ludicrous "old maid" or of promising herself to a man with whom she would find it difficult to carry out her solemn oaths. When Belford, in his capacity as executor of Clarissa's will, questions Anna's intentions toward Hickman, she replies, "I have such an opinion of your sex that I think there is not one man in a hundred whom a woman of sense and spirit can either *honour* or *obey,* though you make us promise both" (4:477). She comments that her own observation of the married state is that even wives who live best have much to bear, and wonders, "*Do you think I ought to marry at all?*" In the conclusion, "supposed to be written by Mr. Belford," we are told that she does indeed marry happily and that the union of "a woman of her fine sense and understanding" to "a man of virtue and good nature" is bound to be happy, especially when the groom's "behaviour to *Mrs. Hickman* is as affectionate as it was respectful to *Miss Howe.*" The reader tends to feel, however, that Anna has settled none too eagerly for the best available. Certainly, the plight of the typical young woman is made clear. Richardson explores this problem further through the character of Charlotte Grandison in his last novel.

As in *Pamela* Richardson makes use of repeated motifs to emphasize themes in *Clarissa.* Again, clothing serves to characterize the heroine, showing her inner qualities through externals. We learn that Clarissa is always beautifully dressed, although, in contrast to the preening Bella, she spends very little time on her toilette. As Lovelace later says, she has "an elegance natural to her" (2:525). When Solmes's courtship is being urged, patterns of silks are sent for from London. "These are the newest, as well as richest, that we could procure" (1:207), Clarissa's mother tells her. Clarissa is to have six new suits, but, with a nice mercantile touch, her father points out that she already has "an entire new suit" and if she chooses to make that part of her trousseau, he will give her "an hundred guineas in lieu." Jewels are also to be bargained for. The eager suitor, Solmes, intends to present her with a set, but if she agrees to have her own, inherited from her grandmother, "new-set, and to make them serve," then "his present will be made in money; a very round sum—which will be given in full property to yourself" (1:207). It is clear that sentiment plays no part in this—either her affection for the memory of her grandmother or the loving desire of her future husband to adorn her bridal beauty. Everything must be new, impressive, and "rich," but, if possible, also a bargain. This, in her mother's eyes, disproves Clarissa's "objection against the spirit of the man" by showing his generosity. It actually demonstrates, of course, that the Harlowes are as mean-spirited as Solmes. Later, Bella will taunt Clarissa with the silks, proffering one after another and suggesting, "*this,* were I you, should be my wedding night-gown" (1:235).

Her clothes are sent to her, grudgingly, after she goes off with Lovelace, only, Bella tells her, because to see them gives her mother pain. Clarissa's habits of neatness and order serve as a defense against Lovelace's encroachments. "Heedlessness and deshabille" are great helps to seduction, Lovelace writes, but "meet her ever so early," Clarissa "is dressed for the day; and at her *earliest hour,* as nice as others dressed" (2:341). He laments that with "all her forms thus kept up," he has made "little progress in the proposed trial." Just as her dress signifies her moral "steadiness" before the rape, so, after it white garments are a sign of her unviolated will. In her first interview with Lovelace, she is dressed in a white damask gown, and even when she is falsely imprisoned for debt in "a horrid hole of a house" her "white flowing robes . . . spreading the dark . . . floor" illuminate the sordid room, a Hogarthian set piece of ruin and squalor. During her final illness, she maintains herself by selling her clothing, gladly parting with these worldly trappings, and looking ever more beautiful "dressed . . . in her virgin white" (4:332).

Again, as in *Pamela,* the garden of Harlowe Place is used to reveal the character of its owners. It is, Lovelace tells us, in the "Dutch taste" implying extensive use of topiary and extreme formality. At the bottom of the garden is an artificial cascade, broken at the beginning of the novel but later mended, and used by Clarissa at one point as a distraction to conceal her own activities. Clarissa's favorite spot in the garden is the "ivy bower" or summer house where she likes to sit while reading or writing. The little pavilion turns its back on the sterile garden of gravel walks and clipped trees, "pointing to a pretty variegated landscape of wood, water, and hilly country, which has pleased her so much that she had drawn it" (1:445). Clarissa is attracted to simplicity and fruitfulness, rejecting the contrivance and artificiality of the Harlowe's pretentious garden. In doing so she also shows herself to have instinctive good taste; she admires a "natural garden" with wide vistas, a preference that had now become the touchstone of true discernment. Clarissa's realm, however, is not the garden at all but the homely henhouse and its yard which is separated from the formal areas by a high yew hedge. Clarissa's hens are of concern to her because they were her grandfather's, left to her care after his death. Bella and James find her care of them ludicrous, but for Clarissa they are a reminder of her beloved grandfather and a link with a more wholesome world of true values. Ironically, the chore of feeding the poultry, a lowly task that no one else will stoop to, enables her to carry on her illicit correspondences with Anna and with Lovelace, using breaks in the brick wall that surrounds the estate.

On two occasions, Clarissa's spiritual separation from the Harlowes is made vividly pictorial as she witnesses family conferences from one side of the hedge. In the first, she tells Anna that "going down to my poultry-yard just now, I heard my brother and sister and that Solmes" (1:266). She is alone on one side of the "high yew hedge . . . which divides the yard from the garden," while they are "laughing and triumphing together" on the other. On another occasion, she begins to walk in the garden, but a servant warns her that the family is coming and her father does not wish to meet her. She hides behind the yew hedge, trembling in apprehension, and hears her father voice her doom as he declares, "Son James, to you, and to Bella, and to you, brother [Uncle Antony] do I wholly commit this matter" (1:411). She has been delivered over to the most hard-hearted of her persecutors. In thinking of escape, Clarissa realizes that the front entrance to the house would be an impossible route with "the young plantations of elms and limes affording yet but little shade or covert." So also the nouveaux riches ambitions of the Harlowes, exemplified by these new plantings, prevent any solution to Clarissa's dilemma that will allow her to retain her proper status, to leave by the front door. Instead, she is forced to think of the back door, which "is seldom opened, and leads to a place so pathless and lonesome" (1:446). There is an oak coppice here, surrounded with ivy and mistletoe, containing the ruins of a chapel, where, fittingly, Lovelace often lurks waiting for letters from Clarissa or news from his spy Joseph Leman. A man once hanged himself in the wood, so it is avoided by the country folk as haunted. It will be through this door that she will leave with Lovelace on her "pathless and lonesome" journey.

Another series of images in *Clarissa* is sexually charged, with knives, keys, keyholes, and open graves suggesting phallic symbolism. They can also be read in a larger context, however, as connoting violation of individual integrity, of the essential core of one's being, what, in fact, the rape signifies for Clarissa. Images of sexuality also combine with images of seeing—mirrors, windows, peep-holes—to produce more complex signifiers that relate to Clarissa's process of self-discovery as well as to Lovelace's spying; and, Cynthia Griffin Wolff has suggested, a third series connects the first two in images related to penetration: on the one hand of intrusion and on the other hand of defense against violation.[12] Clarissa's private spaces, and particularly her letters, become surrogates for Clarissa herself in this conflict. The first physical struggle between Lovelace and Clarissa is over letters, and, as Gillis has pointed out, Richardson carefully prepares for this confrontation by conflating images of privacy.[13] Lovelace tells us that he hankers after "her pockets . . . as the less mischievous attempt" (2:268) and will "never rest until I have discovered . . . her letters" (2:269). He later distracts her by a fervent kiss in order to steal one of her letters, but is forced to relinquish "the ravished paper" (2:272). The escalating duel between Clarissa and Lovelace is signified by his attempts to rifle her most secret hiding places, and by her precautions as she moves her letters from the chest that holds outer clothing to the "wainscot box, which held her linen, and which she put into the dark closet" (2:434).

Early in the novel, Clarissa has a frightful dream. Lovelace, enraged, seizes her, carries her to a churchyard, "and there, notwithstanding all my prayers and tears, and protestations of innocence, stabbed me to the heart, and then tumbled me into a deep grave already dug, among two or three half-dissolved carcasses" (1:433). He then buries her, throwing dirt with his hands and trampling it down with his feet. In one of her disordered writings after the rape, she laments, "O Lovelace! if you could be sorry for yourself I would be sorry too—but when all my doors are fast, and nothing but the keyhole open, and the key of late put into that, to be where you are, in a manner without opening any of them—O wretched, wretched Clarissa Harlowe!" (3:210–11). As Mark Kinkead-Weekes has pointed out, the present tense "are" is especially touching here.[14] Despite all her precautions, despite the fact that her will remained steadfast and that she was drugged into insensibility, Lovelace has succeeded in penetrating her, violating the body that she has been taught to guard and hold sacred. Although she bears no moral responsibility, it has happened; he "is" now within her, and in some sense will always be. Her ultimate triumph is that this emotional consciousness, which Lovelace is confident will subdue and defeat her, is instead overcome by reason based in moral conviction.

Powerful as these trains of imagery are, the effectiveness of *Clarissa* stems principally from Richardson's masterful use of his favored technique of "writing to the moment" with each character speaking in his own voice, unmediated by any editorial or narrative authority. The expanded format of *Clarissa,* as we have seen, gives scope for the epistolary mode to be used with telling effect. As in *Pamela,* the reader is caught up in the action of the novel, with letters interrupted, copied, and eagerly awaited. Letters become the most important thread of Clarissa's life as she becomes more and more isolated, first within the Harlowe house and later at Sinclair's. During the first part of the novel, not only does she depend on letters to Anna and to Lovelace as her only links with the outside world, but she is even forced to communicate with her own family by letter after being denied access to them because of her supposed powers of persuasion. As Terry Castle has pointed out, Clarissa's tragedy can be described as her struggle, and failure, to make her own voice heard.[15] We as readers are given access to these letters and the replies, thereby becoming, like Clarissa, and through her, Anna, interpreters of the documents that both literally compose the novel and fictionally determine its action. As Lovelace's letters play a greater role in the second part of *Clarissa,* the reader gains a privileged position—that of knowing more than either of the principals because we have access to the letters of both—and learns more about the difficulties of interpretation of both writing and behavior. Both Clarissa and Lovelace, denied access to the letters we are privy to, anxiously study each other, not taking words at face value but observing eyes, facial expressions, tone of voice, casual gestures with the most minute care. The broader strokes of *Pamela* had shown that both words and actions could admit of different interpretations, but in *Clarissa* this perception comes to pervade the very fabric of the life of the novel. "What is truth?" said jesting Pilate. The reader must be willing to stay for an answer (*Clarissa* is the longest novel in English), and he must work through to it, undergoing the same doubts, visions, and revisions that form the experience of the characters. Through reading the text our own vision becomes more acute and our judgement more exact.

Dr. Johnson admired this unusual aspect of Richardson's work. Relating how his own reading of the novel had been altered as he progressed through the text, he told Richardson, "You have a trick of laying yourself open to objections, in the first part of your work, and crushing them in subsequent parts."[16]

The reader learns to read the "minutiae," as Richardson put it, exploring the apparently trivial to try to understand how and why humans act as they do. Dr. Johnson, in a famous comparison, declared that while Fielding resembled a man who "could tell the hour by looking on the dial plate," Richardson was "a man who knew how a watch was made."[17] The image of not only seeing the watch with its case removed and its complex interlocking works exposed, but of actually understanding the function and relationship of each delicate gear and spring, is a compelling one. This is the task set for the reader by Richardson's novel, and a task that must be accomplished without the guiding hand of the master clockmaker. The intricate pattern of action and reaction, motives avowed and secret, belief and doubt, truth and falsity is presented as the supposed action actually happens in the words of the characters, the chief actors, themselves. The reader must evaluate those words, and in doing so comes to question the facile way in which we assume an understanding of our own world. Richardson impels us to examine the forces that determine our judgment both of individuals and of society. In *Clarissa* he calls into question the fundamental values of his own world. He shows the difficulties inherent in all human relationships dependent upon fallible apprehensions, and the struggle necessary to achieve spiritual wholeness despite both inner conflicts and external constraints. Most importantly, he graphically presents the tragic waste of human potentiality and fulfillment resulting from the accepted mores of a society that had lost its vision of truth, of justice, and of charity.

Chapter Four
Sir Charles Grandison

After *Clarissa,* Richardson's circle of admirers pressed him to give them the portrait of "a good man—a man who needs not repentance."[1] He had presented two exemplary heroines, but even the reformed Mr. B. was hardly satisfactory as a masculine model. In fact, Richardson declared that one of his express purposes in writing *Clarissa* was to demonstrate the falsity of the "too commonly received notion that a reformed rake makes the best husband" (1:xv). In responding to requests for a true hero, Richardson almost certainly also intended to counteract what he felt was the pernicious influence of Fielding's *Tom Jones*— an attempt, he wrote to the daughters of Aaron Hill, "to whiten a vicious Character, and to make Morality bend to his Practices."[2] The enmity of Richardson toward Fielding undoubtedly originated with *Shamela,* Fielding's parody of *Pamela.* But just as we can credit Fielding with a genuine repugnance toward the values of *Pamela,* and see *Joseph Andrews* not merely as petty literary feuding but rather as an alternative to Richardson's novel both in style and in moral vision, so we should grant Richardson the same right to an honest opinion that "*Tom Jones* is a dissolute book."[3] He was distressed by its popularity, and while jealous pique was undoubtedly a part of this reaction, he did also think that "it had a very bad Tendency."[4] Sir Charles was needed to provide a valid masculine exemplar.

Clarissa, as we have seen, is a tragic vision of true virtue contesting with false but, in worldly terms, overwhelming opposing forces of egotism, aggression, and greed. While Clarissa triumphs as a Christian saint, there is nevertheless a feeling of waste that a young woman of such vibrant potentiality can find no role to play in her corrupt society. *Sir Charles Grandison,* on the other hand, shows us that virtue and happiness are not incompatible in this world in a properly constituted society. Harriet Byron, Richardson wrote to Lady Bradshaigh, was to be "what I would have supposed Clarissa to be, had she not met with such persecutions at home, and with such a tormenter as Lovelace."[5] In her happy marriage to Sir Charles we can see "what might have been" if Clarissa had been fortunate enough to meet a man who was not only good himself but who had the ability to create his own ideal world of love and friendship. *Sir Charles Grandison* is primarily a utopian picture of a society in which virtue indeed produces its own rewards.

The plot of *Grandison* uses the well-worn device of the triangle, here with the hero entangled with two women. In contrast, however, to the usual formula of the worthy woman vying with a corrupt enchantress, Sir Charles is perplexed by having the love of two excellent heroines. The novel begins with Harriet Byron, a beautiful, talented, and much sought-after young woman, leaving her country home in Northamptonshire to come to London with her cousins, the Reeves. We follow Harriet's introduction to the social pleasures of the city through her witty, animated letters back home to Lucy, her best friend, and to the Selbys, the aunt and uncle who have raised her after the death of her parents. She attracts suitors in London just as she had in the country, among them the rake Sir Hargrave Pollexfen, who asks her to marry him. Enraged and incredulous at her refusal, he abducts her after a masquerade, planning a forced marriage. She is rescued, just in time, by the heroic intervention of Sir Charles Grandison. Harriet is soon placed on an intimate footing with Sir Charles's two sisters, Caroline, now Lady L., and Charlotte. Caroline is a model of grave decorum, while Charlotte is witty, vivacious, and assertive. Harriet's gratitude to Sir Charles quickly becomes love, increased by the praises heaped upon him by his sisters, who tell her of his magnanimous conduct toward themselves and others. The sisters detect Harriet's "secret" and favor the match, but Sir Charles himself is enigmatically aloof and often absent. Finally, letters arrive from Italy and we now learn, partly from Sir Charles but chiefly from Dr. Bartlett, his pious mentor, about events of the previous year.

Sir Charles had been dispatched on an extended grand tour by his profligate father who was ashamed to have his son witness his misconduct. While in Italy he bravely rescued Jeronymo Poretta from highwaymen, saving his life, and was subsequently introduced into the grateful Poretta family as a brother. He instructed Clementina, the only daughter, in English, by reading Milton with her. Before she realized what was happening, her gratitude also became love. The Porettas, a powerful, deeply Catholic, aristocratic family were horrified at the idea of Clementina marrying a heretic. They proposed unacceptable terms—Sir Charles must become a Catholic and live in Italy.

He countered with the most generous concessions he was willing to give: the couple will live part of the time in Italy; Clementina will have her own chaplain and perfect freedom to practice her faith; the girls will be brought up as Catholics but the boys will be Protestant. The Porettas refused this compromise, and, obeying their commands, Clementina bade Sir Charles farewell. He soon returned to England because of his father's death. Clementina, however, continues to be tortured by her disappointed love, and this, together with the harsh treatment meted out by a cruel aunt, has driven her into madness. The Porettas now write to Sir Charles, asking him to come back to Italy in the hope that his love will restore Clementina. They are even willing to accept his terms for marriage. Sir Charles feels a deep obligation to Clementina, and, despite the fact that he is obviously attracted to Harriet, he leaves for Italy, deliberately refusing to place her under any obligation whatever.

The next portion of the novel describes Harriet's suspense as she waits for news from Italy. She is in a very uncomfortable position since although her own heart is committed, not only has she had no declaration at all from Sir Charles but it is evident that Clementina has priority. Even if the match falls through, Harriet is afraid she will be only a second choice. She bitterly sums up the possibilities: "if the unhappy Clementina should die; or if she should be buried for life in a nunnery; or if she should be otherwise disposed of; why then, . . . your Harriet may have room given her to hope for a *civil* husband in Sir Charles Grandison, and *half* a heart."[6] While Harriet struggles with her emotions and copes with problems of decorum when she receives a very advantageous offer of marriage from an unexceptionable young lord, Sir Charles awaits Clementina's recovery and maintains the proper dignity of an English Protestant among Italian nobility. Clementina does recover her sanity, and now, fully in possession of her reason and given the power of free choice, she rejects Sir Charles because she fears that her deep love and respect for him, an unregenerate heretic, would endanger her own faith and thereby her salvation.

Clementina's heroic decision is reported, and Sir Charles returns to England to court Harriet. With consummate tact he assures her that she was really his first love, but that he felt a moral obligation to Clementina because of her sufferings and then admiration for her because of her exalted virtue. They marry and Harriet becomes mistress of Grandison Hall to the joy of all. Clementina appears, a fugitive from her family because of their insistence on her marrying Count Belvedere, an eligible and adoring suitor. Sir Charles arranges a compromise between Clementina and her family that presages a probable future marriage to Belvedere, and Sir Charles, Harriet, and Clementina pledge eternal friendship in the garden at Grandison Hall.

Interwoven in the main plot line are the stories of those touched by Sir Charles's gracious benevolence. They include his father's former mistress and her illegitimate children, his best friend Beaumont persecuted by an envious stepmother, his charming ward, Emily Jervois, and her disreputable mother, his stingy and dissolute uncle, a merchant family, the Danbys, and even his former foe, Sir Hargrave Pollexfen. A major subplot deals with the courtship and marriage of Charlotte, his lively sister, by Lord G., a grave but good natured young man. The spectrum of situations presented provides a case book of practical good works and of inquiries into the nature of love—its ideal form and its possible abuses. The novel ends with Harriet expecting their first child, as she and Sir Charles, an ideal couple, serve as the focus for a group of loving friends and relations. Sir Charles has indeed achieved a utopian order based on love in his own private world, and there is a promise that he will soon enter parliament to bring his beneficent influence to the public sphere.

The main problem of the novel, as Richardson himself recognized, is to keep his virtually perfect hero from seeming a prig. "A good man—a man who needs not repentance," he wrote to Lady Bradshaigh, "How tame a character," remarking, "has not the world shewn me, that it is much better pleased to receive and applaud the character that shews us what we are . . . than what we ought to be?"[7] Lady Bradshaigh suggested that what was needed was a good man who nevertheless had the worldly polish and elan of the rake. She quoted to Richardson the description Anna Howe gives of Lovelace at the ball: "So little of the fop; yet so elegant and rich in his dress . . . his air so intrepid: so much meaning and penetration in his face: so much gaiety, yet so little of the monkey . . . no affectation . . . all manly . . . his courage and wit, the one so known, the other so dreaded . . . " (4:24), a figure such that "nobody was regarded but he." Richardson agreed that his hero "must be wonderfully polite; but no Hickman!" and worried whether ladies "will not think a good man a tame man."[8] Lady Bradshaigh also cited *Spectator*, no. 51, "that a man who is *temperate, generous, valiant, chaste, faithful* and *honest,* may, at the same time, have Wit, Humour, Mirth and Good Breeding."[9] Sir Charles, then, was to be endowed with all the panache usually given to the rake in Restoration comedy as well as with all the virtues usually confined to characters who were pious but dull. As Harriet writes to Charlotte, "Did you think of your brother, Lady G., when you once said, that the man who would commend himself to the general favour of us young women, should be a Rake in his address, and a Saint in his heart?" (3:92–93).

Richardson also felt that Sir Charles must not be flawless because, as he wrote to Lady Echlin, "The Character of a mere Mortal cannot, ought not, to be quite perfect."[10] Therefore, he confided to Miss Mulso, "I would draw him as a mortal. He should have all the human passions to struggle with."[11] Despite Richardson's best intentions, however, Sir Charles does emerge as self-consciously punctilious and even complacent. Harriet, somewhat oppressed by the thought of his unfailing prudence, remarks that "He is resolved to have nothing to reproach himself with, in future, that he can obviate at present," and speculates that, "had he been the first man, he would not have been so complaisant to his Eve as *Milton makes Adam*" but rather "he would have done *his own duty,* were it but for the sake of posterity, and left it to the Almighty, if such had been his pleasure, to have annihilated his first Eve, and given him a second" (2:609). Harriet complains of his *"intolerable* superiority," and laments, "I wish he would do something wrong" (2:89).

It is easy to speculate about the difficulties Richardson encountered in creating the character of Sir Charles. An imperfect hero winning through to moral wisdom, like Tom Jones, has great human appeal, as Richardson well knew, but he wished to show that it was possible for a man to be good from the start—"a man who needs not repentance." A good hero oppressed by a wicked world, like Joseph Andrews, also engenders sympathy, but Richardson had already shown persecuted virtue and now wished to demonstrate not only the spiritual rewards of goodness but its practical efficacy when it becomes the basis of worldly dealings. Discarding these two easy formulas for making his protagonist engaging left Richardson with little room for maneuver. More important still, however, may be the fact that he felt slightly in awe of his own creation. Richardson was a diffident man, acutely aware of his own lack of education and his own middle-class status. Sir Charles had to be admirable in every way and therefore is given aristocratic rank, a good classical education, and thorough knowledge of modern languages and of the cultures of Europe, as well as incidental accomplishments such as remarkable musical ability and consummate swordsmanship. Richardson, writing to a friend, declared that when writing his novels he became "absorbed in the character" so that "it is not fair to say—I, identically I, am any-where while I keep within the character."[12] But he also confided that it was difficult for him, "a man obscurely situated, . . . naturally shy and sheepish," to "enter into characters in upper life," and, in the same letter, declared "I own that a good woman is my favorite character."[13] It is probably because of this uneasiness that so few of the letters in *Grandison* are written by Sir Charles himself. The problem of his social status was exacerbated by both codes of manly behavior and his exalted virtue. Harriet, commenting on a rather stiff letter from Sir Charles remarks, "But a woman may be eloquent, from grief and disappointment; when a man, though his nobler heart is torn in pieces, must hardly complain!" (2:608), and Richardson lamented, "there are so many things that may be done, and said, and written by a common man that cannot by a good man, that delicacies arise on delicacies."[14]

The few letters we have from Sir Charles tell us little of any real emotional turmoil. Here again, Richardson's didactic purpose interfered with the psychological realism he had so convincingly created in *Clarissa*. The practical Christian whom Richardson wished to portray always makes a rational choice based upon his best understanding of the moral issues. Once his intelligence has carefully assessed any situation, he follows what his judgment deems to be the best course. Having done this, he has fulfilled his moral duty and leaves the outcome to God's will. This is exactly what Sir Charles does when faced with the dilemma of being loved by two irreproachable women. Clementina has fallen in love entirely without his encouragement, and, indeed, without her own conscious knowledge, which attributes her growing attraction to gratitude until it is too late. Sir Charles feels obligated by his friendship to Jeronymo and by his privileged status in the family to respond as generously as possible. The Porettas, conscious of their wealth and rank, assuming the superiority of the heritors of ancient Rome over the barely civilized English and the certainty of the true faith over heretical Protestantism, never doubt that Sir Charles will be deeply honored by the possibility of such a match. Their arrogant demand that he renounce his religion and his country temporarily frees him, because it is morally unacceptable. On his return to England, however, he prudently guards against any other entanglement until all uncertainty regarding Clementina is resolved. He later tells Harriet, "The moment I saw you . . . I loved you: And you know not the struggle it cost me (my destiny with *our* dear Clementina so uncertain) to conceal my Love" (3:284). But when Clementina is returning to sanity and the Poretta's changed attitude makes marriage possible, his admiration for her virtuous struggle prompts him to feel that "I had not a wish but for . . . Clementina" (3:11), and he comforts himself with the knowledge that Harriet has had a good offer of marriage. He does speculate that, "should Miss Byron be unhappy and through my means, the remembrance of my own caution and self-restraint could not appease the grief of my heart," but quickly reassures himself that this is unlikely "so *prudent* a woman as she is" and so worthy and deserving the Earl of D., her suitor.

While Dr. Bartlett speaks of Sir Charles as being "greatly embarrassed . . . between his honour to one Lady and his tenderness for the other" (2:537), Sir Charles, having made his decision, declares, "To Providence I leave the rest. The result cannot be in my *own* power" (2:382). This is, of course, a properly Christian attitude, but his serene equilibrium is apt to seem just a little too easily achieved. Sir Charles writes to Dr. Bartlett, "What difficulties, my dear friend, have I had to encounter with!" He then, for the reader, calls any moral anguish into question by asserting: "God be praised, that I have nothing, with regard to these two incomparable women, to reproach myself with." Finally, he summarizes his situation with a "we" that perhaps verges on the royal. "I am persuaded that our prudence . . . is generally proportioned to our trials" (2:456). While he has confided that "I have a heart too susceptible for my own peace," he also notes that "I endeavour to *conceal* from *others* those painful sensibilities which they cannot relieve" (2:461). This concealment is fatal. We cannot participate in his struggle, and, since in essence his dilemma is simply which of two equally beautiful and virtuous women providence will decide to give him as a bride, we cannot really feel that his situation merits profound concern.

This problem of easily achieved moral victories continues to affect the reader's reaction to Sir Charles. He is opposed to dueling and, therefore, refuses to engage in any duel, but he has nevertheless trained as a swordsman because he "never could bear a design'd insult" (1:206). He will draw a sword only in self-defense, but when he is forced to do so his skill is such that invariably he disarms his enemy. Sir Charles avows that "I am not so much a coward, as to be afraid of being branded a coward," and, scorning "the empty, the *false* glory, that men have to be thought brave" (1:256), despises the conventions of "honour," asserting "I live not to the world: I live to myself; to the monitor within me" (1:206). This refusal to bow to a convention he regards as wrong is, of course, the mark of true courage and of the good man. The trouble is that it does not cost Sir Charles anything. His physical skill always in fact results in victory, regardless of his refusal to follow convention, and he always gains the respect not only of his opponent but of society in general.

The character in the novel who is faced with a real choice, a choice that involves human loss, is Clementina. She must choose at first between marrying the man she loves to adoration and obeying her family, and later between her love for Sir Charles and her duty to God. Each conflict is ideally suited to the careful exploration of the "divided heart" that was Richardson's forte, but unfortunately, like Mr. B.'s affair with the Countess, the reader experiences Clementina's distress only at second hand. She has no trusted friend to confide in, and the few letters she writes are to Sir Charles himself, necessarily guarded by the protocols of courtship and always the product of careful forethought. The spontaneity, the self-examination, the development of the "minutiae," are all absent. Instead, we have the exterior portrait of a pathetic but remote saint. Even Clementina's kind of piety is apt to estrange the reader rather than attract him. In contrast to Clarissa, who rejected both Solmes and Lovelace because neither was a good man, Clementina rejects a suitor who is indeed a good man, both in her own eyes and when judged by society's standards, solely because of narrow sectarianism. While the novel asks us to admire her choice, and to perceive it as the sincere result of her own commitment, we find it difficult to sympathize fully with a dilemma created solely by an exclusionary doctrine of salvation.

Richardson prefaced his novel with a list of the "Principle Persons" that divides them into "Men," "Women," and "Italians." The classification has become a joke, but it does, nevertheless, indicate something important about the work. Italy here is indeed a world apart. The use of Italy as the realm of heightened emotion, a semifantasy land where people obey the heart rather than the head and where fortuitous coincidence or the *deus ex machina* cuts Gordian knots with ease, has a long and often distinguished tradition in English literature, with Shakespeare the most obvious example. In *Grandison,* however, it works against securing the involvement of the reader which is so important in Richardson's best works. Even Sir Charles, despite his long sojourn on the Continent, never feels at ease with the Porettas—their ways are not his ways. Yet, Richardson's treatment of Roman Catholicism is remarkably tolerant for his time. Clementina's confessor, Father Marescotti, is not portrayed as a sinister monster nor is the mistreatment of Clementina by Laurana, her cousin, and Juliana, her aunt, shown as arising out of inquisitorial motives of misguided faith. Their persecution is based upon jealousy and greed, just as was Bella and James's oppression of Clarissa. Nevertheless, the Poretta's insistence on their own superiority of rank and wealth, on the intrinsic excellence of Italian culture and on the unique status of the Catholic church tends to limit our sympathy for them. Clementina is not exempt from the family pride. In her disordered state, interpreting Sir Charles's refusal to become a Catholic as a pretext for rejecting her, she laments, "Don't let it be told abroad, that a daughter of that best of mothers was refused by any man less than a Prince" (2:206). Sir Charles is willing to make large allowances for all the Porettas, including the insolent elder brother of Clementina and the bigoted bishop, another brother. However, Richardson's contemporaries, despite their admiration for the "divine Clementina," breathed sighs of relief when the good man was saved for England, and even less chauvinistic modern readers are apt to agree.

The pathetic effect of Clementina's madness was much admired by eighteenth-century readers and, indeed, many thought her the finer heroine. (The romantics, not surprisingly, were sure she was superior to the all too sane Harriet.) Modern readers are perhaps more likely to view insanity as an illness that generates concern than as a flight of the soul that arouses esteem. Clementina's derangement, therefore, places another barrier between her and the reader. Clarissa, of course, suffers a temporary loss of reason, but it is short lived, and we witness very little of it aside from the extraordinary "papers" that give us useful insights into her subconscious. Her condition moves us because of the contrast with the perceptive, thoughtful Clarissa we have come to know so well. With Clementina, the reverse is true. We first encounter her in her madness and only learn through retrospective description that once she was an intelligent, lively, witty, altogether sane young woman. Although she "recovers" during the novel, the new balance seems precarious, as her impulsive flight to England indicates.

While Clementina's madness and her essentially alien standards of value tend to estrange the reader, all of this could be overcome if we were given real insight into the difficult choices she has to make. During her derangement we have only secondhand reports. When she recovers, she does write a letter to Sir Charles, refusing him, but we are given only an external description of its composition: "She reads over and over, something she has written; lays it down, takes it up; walks about the room, sometimes with an air of dignity, at others hanging down her head" (2:561). Her family wish that she "shewed greater composure!," and she fusses about which of several dresses to wear for her interview with Sir Charles. Indeed, in contrast to the serene self-assurance of Clarissa in her interview with Lovelace, Clementina's demeanor makes her family fear the "tokens . . . of a disordered, yet a raised mind" (2:561), and, finally, unable to speak, she thrusts upon him "this paper, which has cost me so many tears, so much study, so much blotting-out, and revising and transcribing" (2:565). The reader, however, can only read the final product; he is not allowed to participate in the all-important process that led up to it. A real understanding of the Catholic sensibility that informs Clementina's difficult choice would make us much more sympathetic. Again, when Clementina decides to run off to England our first words from her are, "By this time it is very probable, you have heard of the rashest step that the writer of these presents . . . ever took" (3:332). We learn of her decision only after it has been made, rather than during the crucial intellectual and emotional debate that produced it. Clementina remains always distant from us.

Harriet Byron, on the other hand, is a character whom the reader comes to know well. She is the most extensive letter writer in the novel, and a witty, unassuming, thoroughly engaging young woman. Harriet, however, has few important choices to make. Her early suitors are either too insipid or too rakish to merit serious consideration, and once she meets Sir Charles his every attribute merits her love. There is no struggle here, as in *Clarissa,* between the instinctive attraction of the passions and the forbidding rein of moral judgment. Sir Charles's faultless character justifies the immediate captivation his charm makes inescapable. When Harriet falls headlong in love, her intellectual and moral faculties applaud her choice. Both her own family and Sir Charles's sisters approve the match, and until she learns of Clementina the only cloud on the horizon is Sir Charles's curious aloofness.

Knowledge of Sir Charles's obligations to Clementina changes everything but does not really give Harriet important choices to make, except in the category of decorous deportment. She is still in love with him and certainly while he is unmarried cannot think of another man. Harriet's decisions chiefly concern how to cope with the social embarrassment of being in love with a man who has made no declaration to her. In the courtship customs of the time no "nice young person," as Mrs. Howe phrased it, wished to be thought in love. It was the role of the man to show desire, and by his ardent courtship, hope to awaken some spark in the untouched maidenly heart of his beloved. A girl who languished for a man was an object of derision. Harriet writes to her cousin, "For sex-sake, for example-sake, Lucy, let it not be known to any but the partial, friendly few that [I] have been a volunteer in [my] affections" (2:331). She laments that "Sir Charles Grandison and I have been named together, and talked of, in your neighborhood." With Sir Charles in Italy, her own return home will make her look "*so* silly! So like a refused girl!" and if "Everybody gives him to me" then "So much the worse" (2:331). Her ambiguous state also makes it difficult to respond to a highly advantageous marriage proposal from the Earl of D., not only rich and titled, but "a man of merit" who, Harriet concedes, is "not a disagreeable man in his person and manners" (2:288–89). Because she values honesty over protocol, Harriet does inform the Countess Dowager of D., the young man's mother, of her real situation. She acknowledges that Sir Charles has not made her any offer, and has, indeed, shown "only the same kind of tenderness as he shows to his sisters," but that although "I cannot, and I think, *ought not,* to entertain an hope with regard to Sir Charles Grandison . . . yet is my heart so wholly attach'd, that I cannot think it just to give the least encouragement to any other proposal" (2:289).

Harriet must wait, entirely passive, while her fate is determined. She does not even have the emotional satisfaction of hating her rival. Generous and clear-sighted, Harriet acknowledges Clementina's merits and her prior claim, pities her affliction, and considers that Sir Charles has acted correctly in every sense. She can only pray for resignation, and, indeed, her friends worry as she becomes thin and pale, despite her determined air of cheerfulness and her refusal to indulge in self-pity. Mrs. Selby, Harriet's aunt, warns her that "You are called upon, in my opinion, to a greater trial than ever yet you knew, of that prudence for which you have hitherto been so much applauded" (1:213), but, in truth, the trial is one of suitable deportment, not of moral conflict. Harriet's head approves the choice of her heart, and now she can only await the decision of providence.

Symptomatic of the generally lower level of emotional intensity characteristic of *Grandison* is the nature of the letters themselves. In *Pamela* and *Clarissa* letters served as emotional lifelines as Pamela reaches out to her parents and Clarissa to Anna Howe. The letters are hidden, smuggled, intercepted, forged, and subjected to careful scrutiny and interpretation: finally, they influence the action of the novel itself. Privacy, secrecy is usually their hallmark and near desperation is often their tone. In *Grandison,* letters are communal and public. When Harriet first comes to London, she writes back to her cousin Lucy in Northamptonshire, but with the understanding that her letters will be shared with the whole Selby family—her aunt and uncle, grandmother Shirley, cousin Nancy, and, it seems, any friends or neighbors who drop in. There is, of course, a moral point to be made—Harriet writes to Lucy, "But you and I, my dear, write for all to see what we write" (1:178), and we remember that Clarissa bitterly reproached herself for continuing a clandestine correspondence with Lovelace—but the atmosphere of confidential disclosure is lost. Later in the novel, Harriet's letters to Charlotte are shared with another family circle. Sir Charles's letters from Italy are written to Dr. Bartlett, but again, with the understanding that they will be communicated to the whole family. Indeed, even letters one might assume to be private, such as Sir Charles's reply to Pollexfen's challenge, are shown about, first to Harriet's cousin Reeves, then to her, then transcribed by her (without permission) and sent down to the "venerable circle" at Selby Hall, and so on. Letters are continually copied, with or without permission, sent on for others to read, and generally handed about as public property. The novel begins with Lucy obtaining a letter from one of Harriet's suitors that describes Harriet. "He seemed to make a scruple of *your* seeing it," she writes Harriet, "but it was a faint one." His "faintness" is immediately interpreted as permission, and, when, before showing Lucy the letter, he asks for ink to scratch out certain passages "with so many little flourishes (as you will see) that he thought they could not be read" (1:8), she cleverly brings him a pale ink so that they are still "legible by holding up the letter to the light" (1:10). A group that exhibits the greatest punctilio in delicate questions of propriety seems to have no ethics at all with regard to private correspondence. The word "private" loses all significance in the novel when applied to letters, and the reader's sense of intimate emotional involvement with the writers diminishes as well.

This total lack of secrecy, this sunlit world of openness and candor, which differs so markedly from the claustrophobic world of *Clarissa,* also indicates the main theme of *Grandison.* Here we are to experience not so much the interior world of "the divided heart" as the social world of practical Christianity drawing all into its blessed circle. Sir Charles, Richardson declared, was to be "happy in himself, and a Blessing to others" (1:4). *Grandison* was Jane Austen's favorite novel. Her nephew reports, "Every circumstance narrated in Sir Charles Grandison, all that was ever said or done in the cedar parlor, was familiar to her; and the wedding days of Lady (Grandison) and Lady G. were as well remembered as if they had been living friends."[15] While George Eliot, another admirer, wrote of *Grandison*: "I had no idea that Richardson was worth so much. . . . The morality is perfect—there is nothing for the new lights to correct."[16] It is reasonable to suppose that it was the more normative atmosphere of the novel, the exploration of subtleties of social behavior that made *Grandison* so valuable to these two great novelists. The weaknesses of the novel are generally related to its lack of emotional tension, but its strengths become evident if we approach it as an idealized picture of a society where virtue rules. Sir Charles is not only good in himself, but sufficiently powerful and sagacious to create a virtual utopia within his sphere. In this charmed circle we are privileged to explore how life ought to be lived, rather than making do with the imperfections offered by the everyday world.

In Harriet, Richardson presents us with his ideal woman, happily free of the constraints that inhibited Clarissa. She is, of course, beautiful, but even Greville, a rakish suitor, asks who "can describe the person of Miss Harriet Byron, and her person only; animated as every feature is by a mind that bespeaks all human excellence?" (1:9), and declares that "lovely as Miss Byron's person is, I defy the greatest sensualist on earth not to admire her mind more than her person." Harriet is older than Richardson's other heroines, twenty when the novel opens, and the most independent. She is an orphan who has been raised by a loving aunt and uncle, the Selbys, together with her grandmother, Mrs. Shirley. While she is not wealthy, Harriet's moderate inheritance obviates any financial worries, and her judgment has proved so prudent that her guardians have given her complete discretion in choosing her future husband. Harriet's position is thus completely the reverse of the typical young woman of the eighteenth century who was totally dependent on her parents. The kind of autonomy granted to Harriet was generally considered a grave danger by the writers of conduct books who proclaimed that the weaker sex needed the strong guiding hand of the rational male to direct her frail intellects and to check her wayward emotions, so prone was she to deception by specious villains and to temptation by her own unregulated passions. Much of the fiction of the period consists, in fact, of morality tales demonstrating that young women who strive for the freedoms given to Harriet come to bad ends, or, perhaps more frequently, are saved in the nick of time by a male who then restores the proper status quo, usually by marriage. Harriet, on the contrary, justifies the trust placed in her by acting meritoriously in every situation.

Harriet's conduct is always guided by standards of truthfulness and by a determination to cause as little pain to others as is humanly possible. When social custom is at variance with these goals, Harriet disregards protocol and acts according to her own values. In doing so, she demonstrates her affinity to Sir Charles who also places moral imperatives above social conventions, as we have seen in his refusal to duel. Sir Charles is so scrupulous that he refuses to "pervert the meaning of words" and he "never, for instance, suffers his servants to deny him, when he is at home" (2:388). So also Harriet eschews the "delicacies" of feminine deportment in favor of honesty, and, in the case of the Earl of D., frankly reveals that she is in love with Sir Charles rather than keeping him in suspense while sheltering behind the enigmatic mask that decorum permits. In all her decisions, Harriet follows reason. Her greatest temptation in the novel is that of being unjust in her attitude toward her rival, Clementina. As her love for Sir Charles wars with the moral imperative to treat Clementina with "generosity, or rather, justice," Harriet finds "my heart [pulled] two ways" (2:300). She exhorts herself, "Harriet Byron . . . be not mean," and reflects, "Sir Charles Grandison is just: He *ought* to prefer . . . the excellent Clementina," naming as reasons priority, compassion, and her rival's merits, and then asks, "I love him for *his* merits: Shall I not love merits nearly as great in my own sex?" Admitting that the struggle will be difficult, she adjures herself, "Often have I contended for the dignity of my own sex; let me now be an example to myself," and, she writes to Lucy, "However hard it is to prefer another to one's self, in such a case as this; yet if my judgement is convinced, my acknowledgement shall follow it" (2:366). Trusting, like Sir Charles, to providence, she declares, "Heaven will enable me to be reconciled to the event, because I pursue the dictates of that judgement, against the biasses of my more partial heart." We never learn whether Harriet would indeed entirely succeed in her goal of subduing passion to reason, but her own pride encourages her to strive so that "*my* conquest of my passion is at least as glorious for me," as Sir Charles's conduct has been, since "I can most sincerely, however painfully, subscribe to the preference which

Honour, Love, Compassion, unitedly give to CLEMENTINA" (2:387).

Especially in the early part of the novel, Harriet's clear vision provides a light by which others are judged. Much to his own astonishment, the rakish fop, Sir Hargrave Pollexfen, far from arousing the awed admiration that his own frequent glances in the mirror assure him he deserves, is at first an object of amusement to Harriet, and when he persists in his attentions, an annoyance. His self-satisfied assurance is an indication of the advantage held by men in courtship at this time, both because women of marriageable age outnumbered them and because marriage was really the only acceptable career for women.[17] "I did not believe I should have been rejected by any lady, who had no dislike to a change of condition; and was disengaged," Pollexfen declares, citing, "my *person*, my *fortune*, my *morals*, my *descent*, my *temper*" as all "unexceptional" (1:113). He even condescends to kneel to Harriet, who gravely points out that since "you have great reason to be satisfied with *your*-self" he should be able to understand that she must act so as to "leave me as well satisfied with *my*-self."

Harriet never seeks the limelight, but when she is called upon to speak she is eloquent. Sir Charles notes that her fine mind is "legible in her face" and asks, "Have you not observed . . . what intelligence her very silence promises?," adding, "And yet, when she speaks, she never disappoints the most raised expectation" (1:424). Harriet always speaks up for women, and when someone begins to praise her as being different from the generality, she interrupts, saying, "You must know that I never can accept of any compliment that is made me at the expence of my sex" (1:40).

On one occasion she is called upon to debate with an Oxford pedant, Mr. Walden, who holds that no one can be considered learned who is not versed in Greek and Latin. Knowledge of the classics was the foundation of higher education in the eighteenth century, and, as noted above, women were generally excluded from this knowledge both because they were denied access to the universities and because such studies were thought too difficult. Proponents for the intellectual equality of the sexes tended to follow two different lines of reasoning. The first contended that women were perfectly capable of such learning and that this accomplishment would not unfit them for their role in life, but rather improve them as companions for their husbands. Miss Clements, who has been described by Harriet as "plain; but of a fine understanding, improved by reading" (1:42), takes this position, asking, "Is it a *necessary* consequence, Sir, that knowledge which makes a man shine, should make a woman vain and pragmatical?" (1:49), and opining that "two persons, having the same taste [may] improve each other." The other argument questioned the importance of knowing Greek and Latin as an index of true learning. Harriet implies this position when she asks, with an air of assumed innocence, which languages he considers learned (she is herself a "perfect mistress" of French and Italian). She then points out "that a learned man and a linguist may be two persons" and that "knowledge, and not language merely is learning" (1:51). Further, she takes the side of the moderns against the ancients. She traps Walden into admitting that learning is "a progressive thing," and that "skill in languages [is] a *vehicle* to knowledge," not "*science* itself" and asks, "have not the moderns . . . if they have equal genius's, the same heavens, the same earth, the same works of God, or of *nature,* as it is called, to contemplate upon and improve by?" (1:52). Furthermore, the moderns have the advantage not only of knowing the ancients but of recent discoveries in science and, most important of all, "a Revelation from Heaven," so that their works are not grounded on "Pagan . . . foolishness" (1:54). Harriet concedes a "great respect even for linguists," in part because they have translated the Bible, but objects when the "confusion of tongues, which was intended for a punishment of presumption in the early ages of the world," is now "thought to give us our greatest glory in these *more enlightened* times" (1:55). Mr. Walden's shallow pedantry is effectively challenged, although Harriet will later admire the unostentatious learnedness of Sir Charles. The question is summarized by Harriet's wise Grandmother Shirley, at another time, when she declares that "women are generally too much considered as a species apart" and that superiority in learning is not "founded on a natural difference of capacity" but rather on differences in opportunity. The same lack of opportunity, she points out, often prevents many men in demanding professions from acquiring scholarly attainments, but this does not mean that such men are to be scorned. "A learned man . . . who should despise a sensible one of these professions . . . would pass for a pedant," she declares, asking, "and why not for despising or undervaluing a woman of sense, who may be put on the same footing?" (3:244).

Harriet, then, is a young woman who has not merely beauty but wit and sense together with virtue. Unlike Clarissa, she is fortunate enough to meet and marry a man who is her equal in every respect. In Charlotte, Sir Charles's sister, Richardson explores the difficulties of a young woman who is not quite so lucky. The problems an intelligent

woman faced in finding a suitable husband whom she could honestly
promise to honor and obey had been explored in *Clarissa* through the
courtship of Anna Howe and Hickman. Their story was necessarily
subordinated to Clarissa's own trials, however, and their marriage is
merely summarized in a sentence or two from Belford. In Charlotte's
more fully developed story we follow not only the courtship but the
ensuing marriage. When the novel begins Charlotte is uncomfortably
entangled with an unworthy suitor. Sir Charles manages to free her
from this engagement, but, convinced that marriage is the best route
to happiness for a woman, urges her to marry. She is sought by Lord
G., a good-natured, affable young man who is much in love with her,
but who, unfortunately, is not her equal in intelligence. "Am I con-
ceited, Harriet?," she asks, "Which of the two silly folks do you think,
has most (Not wit—Wit is a foolish thing, but) understanding? I *think*
the woman has it, all to nothing" (2:553). She is correct, and her
dilemma was certainly one faced by many bright young women. As
Harriet sums up the situation, "What can a woman do, who is addressed by a man of talents inferior to her own?," observing, "She
cannot pick and choose, as men can. She has only her negative; and, if
she is desirous to oblige her friends, not always *that*" (1:230). She notes
that "it is said, women . . . must encourage Men of Sense only. And
it is well said," and then complains, "But what will they do, if their
lot be cast only among Foplings? If the Men of Sense do not offer
themselves?" The alternative, of course, was spinsterhood, and ridicule
of "old maids" is condemned in the novel. Harriet chides Charlotte for
some sharp descriptions of her unmarried aunt, declaring, "I think it
looks like a want of decency in women, to cast reflections on others of
their Sex, possibly for their prudence and virtue" (2:662), and warns
her that such ridicule in fact exalts the power of men, making them
indeed "Lords of Creation." Nevertheless, Mrs. Shirley, Harriet's wise
grandmother, speaks for the age when she describes the life of a spinster. "A single woman is generally an undefended, unsupported creature," she says, "Her early connections, year by year, drop off; no new
ones arise; and she remains solitary and unheeded, in a busy bustling
world" (3:397).

Those women who cannot find their ideal husband, are, therefore,
better off settling for second best, and Sir Charles advises Charlotte,
"If you cannot have a man of whose understanding you have an higher
opinion than of your own, you should think of one who is likely to
allow to yours a superiority" (2:99). Sir Charles is explicitly reversing

the marital values that formed the accepted code of conduct for the century. As Clarissa so strongly asserted, the marriage vows to honor and obey presuppose a superiority on the part of the husband. Charlotte's marriage to Lord G. clearly embodies the reverse, and, through the happy resolution of their difficulties suggests a new standard of companionship rather than authority as the basis for mutual and long continuing love. Charlotte is frank in admitting "I know not what Love is" (2:517), but, as Harriet observes, "She hates not Lord G. There is no man whom she prefers to him," adding, "and in this respect may, perhaps, be on a par with eight women out of twelve, who marry, and yet make not bad wives" (2:347).

Charlotte accepts, and while the couple eventually do attain great happiness, we are given a lively picture of some of the difficulties inherent in such a match. "For the man one loves," Charlotte observes somewhat wistfully, "one can *do* anything, *be* everything, that he would wish one to be" (2:340), but Lord G. seems to persist in reminding her of his limitations. She confides in Harriet that "he is so important about trifles; so nimble, yet so slow: He is so sensible of his own *intention* to please, and has so many antic motions in his obligingness, that I cannot forbear laughing" (2:417). He is one of those maddening people who never quite sees the point of an objection. When Charlotte disparages his "gew-gaw taste" for fashionable trifles, he offers to give away his butterfly collection, but, she says to Harriet, "by what study, thought I, wilt thou . . . supply their place?" (2:417). Lord G. is fond of neither reading nor writing although Charlotte concedes he "spells pretty well, for a Lord" (2:419). Hoping to please his captious bride, Lord G. presents her with a tea set of fine "old Japan China." She describes him "busying himself with taking out, and putting in the windows, one at a time, the cups, plates, jars, and saucers, rejoicing and parading over them, and shewing his connoisseurship to his motionless admiring wife," until he claims the "*liberty,* as he phrased it," of a kiss and then paced backward "several steps with such a strut and crow" (2:418). She confesses, "I burst into a hearty laugh; I could not help it," and while Lord G. looks perplexedly to see if there is anything amiss in his dress, "The man . . . I could have said . . . is the oddity! Nothing amiss in the garb . . . but had too much reverence for my husband."

As Harriet clearly perceives, if Lord G. would only "assume dignity" yet still be able "to laugh *with* her and sometimes *at* her" (2:330), then all would be well, but instead Charlotte's philosophy is "What a duce shall a woman marry a man of talents not superior to her own, and forget to reward herself for her condescension?" (2:321), declaring, "I love to jest, to play, to make him look about him" (2:506). While Charlotte's playfulness borders sometimes on childish and sometimes on cruel behavior, we do nevertheless understand how the unwitting, pompous triviality of her husband provokes it. At last, she realizes that she is pursuing the wrong path, and that she had best "retreat . . . with honour, before harden[ing] the man's heart" (2:518). Now, she reports to Harriet, "I have told him, in love, some of his foibles: And he thanks me for my instruction, and is resolved to be all I wish him to be" (2:543), while she comments that "I have made discoveries in his favour—More wit, more humour, more good sense, more learning." She points herself out to Harriet as "an example of true conjugal fidelity," noting that she is, therefore, "an encouragement for girls who venture into the married state, without that prodigious quantity of violent passion, which some hare-brained creatures think an essential of Love" (3:402). Charlotte ends by declaring, "You, my dear, left us *tolerably* happy. But now we are now almost *in*-tolerably so."

Charlotte's marriage is certainly intended to show that happiness could result from unions based on prudence rather than passion, but it also suggests that good marriages could be based upon models different from the conduct book standard of patriarchal authority. Charlotte has always made it clear that while she does not love Lord G. passionately, she never would have married him if she did not give him preference over all other men. (Sir Charles is an exception here, but *hors concours* because he is her brother.) Charlotte simply refuses to "dwindle into a wife." She wishes to keep her characteristic wit and liveliness, the qualities after all, that presumably attracted Lord G. She has declared, "I am not absolutely ungenerous. If he can but show his love by forbearance, I will endeavour to reward his forbearance with my love" (2:506). This is what happens, almost to her surprise. Sir Charles's insight that a woman like Charlotte who will find it very difficult to meet her peer had better then marry a man who will "allow to [her wit] a superiority" is correct, and while the resulting marriage certainly does not reflect the usual pattern of submission and dominance, it does result in improving both—Charlotte learns to control her willfulness, while Lord G. gains dignity and good sense. The extremes of Charlotte's behavior are condemned by Sir Charles, Harriet and all the good characters, but the basic pattern of the marriage is not. In fact, when a foolish cousin, Everard Grandison, marries a wealthy bourgeoise, Sir Charles comments ironically on the match, noting that "she has a greater opinion of his understanding than she has of her own." While Sir Charles clearly thinks it nearly impossible that anyone could equal, let alone excel, Everard in stupidity, he declares "I am glad of it," explaining, that belief in the husband's superiority "seems to be necessary to the happiness of common minds in wedlock" (3:348). The inference, of course, is that better minds can accept greater truth in marriage, rather than slavish adherence to convention.

A number of other matches show that prudence and virtue can produce happiness even when passionate love is missing. Harriet, in fact, deplores the role of "fancy," declaring that "those who marry while it lasts, are often disappointed of that which they propose so largely to themselves: while those who wed for convenience and deal with tolerable honesty by each other, are at a greater certainty" (2:333). Sir Charles arranges a marriage of convenience between his formerly dissolute uncle, Lord W., and a poor, deserving spinster, Miss Mansfield, making sure that both parties enter into the union with open eyes, aware that neither is passionately in love. The marriage is indeed a success, so much so that Charlotte says that not even her brother and Harriet are happier than this couple, declaring, "people may be *very* happy, if not *most* happy, who set out with a moderate stock of Love, and supply what they want in that, with Prudence" (3:228).

While some arranged marriages are approved, forced marriages are condemned. Sir Charles urges Charlotte to make what he considers a desirable match, but he is clear that he would never ask her to marry against her will. He tells his good friend Beauchamp, whom he hopes to match with his ward Emily, "Let me add, that Emily shall give signs of preferring you to all men, as I expect from you demonstrations of your preferring her to all women; or I shall make a difficulty, for both your sakes, of giving a guardian's consent" (3:347). Both Sir Charles and Harriet are distressed when the Poretta family, after Clementina's refusal of Sir Charles, bring pressure upon her to marry a highly eligible suitor, the Count of Belvedere. In a scene reminiscent of *Clarissa,* Clementina's brother demands, "Shall a father kneel in vain? . . . Shall a mother in weeping silence in vain entreat?—Now, my sister, comply" (3:59). When Harriet is reassured that "they will not *compel* her, " she indignantly replies, "Persuasion, Sir, in the circumstances this excellent lady is in, is a compulsion" (3:310), and when she is told that "the Count adores her," she angrily retorts, "*Adores her,* Sir! Adores *himself* !," arguing, as Clarissa vainly argued, that a man who truly loves will prefer "the happiness of the object beloved, to his own." Family pressure eventually impels Clementina to flee to England, and Sir Charles then secures an agreement whereby Clementina will be left in peace for one year. Both Sir Charles and Harriet agree that the Count would make a good husband for Clementina, and that it is indeed preferable that she marry, so the emphasis on the Poretta's wrongheadedness serves to make it clear that forcing a young woman to marry is bad even if the match itself is desirable and the parents' motives are benevolent. On another occasion, Sir Charles declares, "There is hardly any-thing gives me more pain, than when I see a worthy woman very unequally yoked" (2:45). One of the charities he is "most intent upon promoting" is giving dowries to young maidens so that they may marry "with honest men of their own degree" (2:11), while another is a scheme for a kind of Protestant nunnery[18] "in which single women of small or no fortunes" might, by joining together, be able "to maintain themselves genteelly" and "to accomplish all manner of good works" (2:355–56). Such a refuge would benefit those who marry only because "the state of a single woman [is] here so peculiarly unprovided and hopeless."

The ideal marriage, of course, is one of great love on both sides. In the novel the happiness of Sir Charles and Harriet is prefigured by that of Lord L. and Lady L., formerly Caroline Grandison, Sir Charles's other sister. Harriet remarks, "This was a match of love, and does honour to it" (1:210). In their courtship, however, Lord L. declares to his future wife that while "you are dearer to me than my life . . . my love, madam, has *friendship* for its base," and although "*love* might be selfish; . . . *friendship* could not" (1:332). It is clear from Sir Charles's amorous impatience before the marriage—he surprises Harriet at one point with a fervid, "downright" kiss—and the behavior of the happy pair on the wedding night, that sexuality is an important ingredient in true wedded bliss, but what is stressed as most important is the mutual respect that the term "friendship" implies. Lord and Lady L., for example, each hold a key to their money drawer, and each is free to take whatever is needed, noting the withdrawal in a memorandum book. When Everard Grandison, the foolish cousin, maintains that for women marriage is a state "of servitude, if they know their duty" and that women should "stand in awe" of their husbands, Lady L. jokingly asks Lord L. why "you seem not to think it worth your while to *overawe* me," and is answered by Charlotte that "none but rakes hold these *over-awing* doctrines" because they know their own worthlessness and, "having the hearts of slaves, they become tyrants" (1:299). The history of Sir Charles's father and mother serves as an example of the perversion of love that a tyrannical marriage produces. The faultless Lady Grandison bears with her husband's selfishness and debauchery, living in uncomplaining penury and dying an early death hastened by grief. The daughters then become the victims of their father's improvidence and cruelty when he forbids them to marry unless they can do so to his financial advantage, that is, virtually sell themselves on the marriage market, exchanging an aristocratic connection for ready cash. Only his death rescues them, and Sir Charles, despite the somewhat embarrassed condition of the estate, makes it his first concern to assure his sisters, who are totally dependent upon his generosity, that "the moment I can, I will give you an absolute independence on your brother," saying he is sorry "for your *spirits* sake, that you are left in my power" (1:374).

The marriage of Sir Charles and Harriet is a true example of all that a loving union should be. The keynote of their marriage is complete trust based upon mutual admiration of each other's mental and moral qualities. Sir Charles, in describing Harriet, notes that for most men her first attraction is her beauty, but he sees "A mind great and noble: A sincerity beyond that of women: A goodness unaffected, and which shews itself in action . . . A wit lively and inoffensive: And an understanding solid and useful" (2:10). Sir Charles "is valued by those who know him best, not so much for being an handsome man; not so much for his birth and fortune; nor for this or that single worthiness; as for being, in the great and yet comprehensive sense of the word, *a good man*" (1:182). Harriet has found the man Clarissa was seeking, a husband she could truthfully vow to love, honor, and obey. Sir Charles, however, insists that in their marriage these obligations should be mutual. When Harriet jokes about having sovereignty during "her" time—the time of courtship when the woman's word was law—Sir Charles declares, "*mine* will never come. Every day, to the end of my life, will be yours" (3:129). He promises, "I will not take any important step, whether relative to myself or friends, but by your advice" (3:346), and declares, "In everything . . . shall your wishes determine mine" (3:175), insisting, "I want [you] to have a will, and to let me know it" (3:252).

Sir Charles's behavior as a husband is the practical application of his attitudes toward women in general, and his corresponding attitudes toward what properly constitutes the male ideal. He differs from the prevailing modes of his society, both patriarchal and libertine, that

Richardson had exposed in *Clarissa*. Sir Charles believes, with Harriet, that "men and women are . . . much alike . . . put custom, tyrant custom out of the question." Women are intelligent fellow humans who should be treated with the same respect as men. When Sir Charles talks with women, we are told, he avoids the empty gallantry that in fact demeans women's understanding and "addresses himself to women, *as* women, not as goddesses; yet does honour to the persons and to the sex" (3:139). He deplores the double standard, asking, "How can that crime be thought pardonable in a man, which renders a woman infamous?" (2:140), and Dr. Bartlett testifies that Sir Charles's own virtue "is virtue upon *full proof,* and against sensibilities, that it is heroic to overcome," adding "Lady Olivia knows this" (2:326). (Lady Olivia is a beautiful, wealthy, aristocratic Italian who, passionately in love with Sir Charles, offers herself to him "without conditions." The incident, Richardson explained to Lady Bradshaigh, was specifically designed to demonstrate his hero's chastity.) While Sir Charles is described as completely fulfilling the heroic ideal—he is brave, handsome, a good swordsman, a skillful rider, physically strong, gallant, and polite—he rejects the stereotypical manifestations of this role—dueling, displaying his power, making men fear and women love him. Instead, as Harriet says, "his is the gentlest of manly minds" (2:375). When Harriet falls seriously ill, Sir Charles becomes her nurse. "He stirred not from my chamber for half an hour together, for two whole days and nights," she reports, and "every cordial, every medicine, did he administer to me with his own hands," giving still new proof of "his tender goodness" (3:421). In the Grandison circle, whether in London, at Harriet's home in Northamptonshire, or eventually at Grandison Hall, we see a society of men and women coming together on an equal footing, participating in intellectual discussion on questions of morals and manners, united by friendship and mutual respect.

Sir Charles's many charities show him observing not merely the letter of the law, what "is," but rather that which his Christian sense of benevolence prompts, what "ought to be."[19] Thus, although his good friend Mr. Danby has left Sir Charles a fortune in gratitude for saving his life and in admiration of his sterling qualities, Sir Charles feels it only right to restore the money to Danby's disappointed relatives, two nephews and a niece, explaining, "I never will be a richer man than I ought to be" (1:455). The young people are astounded by his generosity and he asks them not to thank him, since benevolence brings its

own reward, but "to do good to your fellow-creatures . . . and in all
your transactions, to *remember mercy,* as well as *justice."* Even the lawyer,
Mr. Sylvester, who has at first congratulated Sir Charles on his "wind-
fall" and assured him that the nephews will be ready to sign a quit-
claim, is so touched that he now plans to look over his own affairs to
see if he can "do some little good, after such a *self-rewarding* example"
(1:456). The incident shows how an individual, without making any
heroic sacrifice, can obey the dictates of Christian charity and by his
private actions not only change lives but begin a chain reaction of
benevolence.[20] In the "Concluding Note" to *Sir Charles Grandison,*
Richardson replied to the criticism that his hero was too faultless by
pointing out that "he performs no one action which it is not in the
power of any man in his situation *to* perform" (3:464), and the emphasis throughout the novel is on the good that can be accomplished by a
man who lives in society, but whose "Actions are regulated by one
steady Principle: A Man of Religion and Virtue," who is "happy in
himself, and a Blessing to others" (1:4).

On other occasions, tact is of greater importance than munificence.
Here, Sir Charles is expert in applying the concept of the ruling passion. The philosophy and psychology of the day taught that man
achieved inner harmony not by ignoring or subduing his passions and
self-love, which were an essential part of his humanity, but by bringing
them into harmony with reason, the proper governor of his actions,
and with social love, the inherent need for others. Each individual has
one "ruling passion" which, properly directed, will result in the most
complete development of his nature—pride, envy, even lust, if turned
into the proper channel, can become a means to virtue.[21] Thus, Sir
Charles recognizes that his uncle Lord W. is a sensualist who chiefly
desires his own ease and comfort. He returns him to the paths of virtue
simply by helping him get rid of a troublesome mistress and by finding
him an agreeable wife who will make his life much more pleasant. Lady
Beauchamp, on the other hand, the jealous stepmother of his good
friend, Edward, is motivated by pride, envy, and greed. She fears her
husband's son as a rival both for his affections and his fortune. Here,
Sir Charles uses flattery, praising her for "graces that . . . appeared but
faintly . . . till his compliments lighted them up, and made them
shine full out" (2:334). He creates for her a self-image of a gracious,
benevolent benefactor, distributing benefits with lavish nobility and
reaping the praise and love of all who know her. Harriet records Sir
Charles's technique, describing how "she took to herself, and *bridled*

upon it, . . . the praises and graces this adroit manager gave her" (2:334). Her vanity now prompts her to treat Edward generously. The mother of his ward, Emily Jervois, presents another problem. Mrs. Jervois is a coarse, dissolute woman who can only be held in check through fear. Sir Charles makes it clear to her and her new "husband" that correct behavior will be rewarded by liberal financial support but that he will not be intimidated by bullying threats. His sweet young ward can then have the pleasure of treating her wayward mother generously without the danger of encouraging ever more outrageous encroachments. The good Christian and the practical man unite in Sir Charles.

Dress is again used in *Grandison* as emblem, although, in keeping with the open, social nature of the novel, its significance here is consonant with generally accepted values, rather than any private or subliminal meanings. Harriet's masquerade dress is a good example. She is costumed in the dress of "an Arcadian Princess," but, as Harriet says, "it falls not in with any of my notions of the Pastoral dress of Arcadia" (1:115). It is very showy, with silver fringe and spangles that make "a mighty glitter," while a close fitting waistcoat displays her "shape" and a net cap is adorned with "a chaplet of artificial flowers, with a little white feather perking from the left ear." The dress is, of course, the exact opposite of the simplicity suggested by the term "arcadian," but fully in keeping with the false values epitomized by the masquerade itself. Ironically, Harriet's natural beauty and unaffected candor make her well suited to the idyllic golden age of prelapsarian virtue, but the costume itself effectively denies her true nature and suggests the shallow flirt. When Sir Hargrave Pollexfen abducts her, planning a forced marriage, the white and silver of the dress become a parody of bridal finery, a wedding gown as false as the ceremony itself. Harriet blushes whenever she recalls that Sir Charles's first view of her was "dressed out, like a fantastic wretch" (1:168). Her actual wedding garb, when she marries Sir Charles, is "the least shewy. All in Virgin white," and "She looks, she moves, an Angel!" (3:219). Her true nature is fulfilled in this happy marriage, and the contrast is recalled to our minds by Charlotte, who reports "No *impediments* were confessed by either of the parties," and comments, "I suppose this reference would have been omitted by Sir Hargrave's snuffling Parson" (3:226).

Sir Charles's customary dress, as might be expected, is carefully considered. He explains to Harriet, "In my own dress, I am generally a conformist to the fashion" (3:124). Admitting that "I rather perhaps dress too shewy," he explains that "my father loved to be dressed" and that he tries to tread in "all my father's steps, in which I could tread," following his father's example "in matters which regard not morals." Good taste is the outward sign of good judgment, and we find Charlotte and Lady L., like Harriet, dressed with quiet elegance, whereas Lady Beauchamp reveals her thirst for admiration by overly elaborate gowns and Mrs. Jervois shows her debased nature by outright tawdriness. Clementina's dress reflects her state of mind, disordered when she is mad and dignified when she is herself. As we have seen above, her difficulty in choosing a dress for the all-important interview with Sir Charles betrays her agitation, and significantly, her final choice of plain white prefigures Harriet's wedding dress, although she has specifically discarded a gown of white and silver, reminiscent of Harriet's masquerade costume, as too bridal in appearance. Other characters advertise their idiosyncracies through their dress—Sir Rowland Meredith's old-fashioned brass buttons, for example, or Sir Hargrave's excessively foppish "brocaded sides."

More important in the novel is the use of house and garden as an emblem of the owner. As we have seen, Mr. B.'s garden embodies the virtues and defects of Mr. B. himself, while the grounds of Harlowe Place illustrate the showy pretentiousness and the unnatural coldness of the Harlowes. Grandison Hall and its surrounding acres form an idealized picture of the English country house as a pattern of harmony and virtue. Harriet, looking out from her new home, declares, "The gardens and lawn seem from the windows of this spacious house to be as boundless as the mind of the owner, and as free and open as his countenance" (3:272). Lucy Selby gives us a description of the park that demonstrates the harmony of old and new, man and nature, beauty and use, fancy and decorum. Here we see a paradigm of all that the age hoped to find in the Horatian ideal of the country gentleman who eschewed "austerity . . . on one hand; ostentation, affectation on the other," displaying instead "Such a glorious benevolence! Such enlarged sentiments!" (3:140). Lucy begins, "This large and convenient house is situated in a spacious park" (3:272). With "large" significantly linked with "convenient" we are immediately in the lineage of Jonson's Penshurst, built for use, not envious show. In the park we find "a noble cascade" that is far removed from the pretension of the Harlowe's puny artiface, as it "tumbles down its foaming waters from a rock, which is continued to some extent, in a kind of ledge of rock-work rudely disposed." Here nature is skillfully augmented by the hand of man. Sir

Charles "delights to preserve, as much as possible, the plantations of his ancestors," but has also opened and enlarged "many fine prospects" and since "the whole [is] bounded only by sunk fences, the eye is carried to views that have no bounds" (3:273). The walls that constricted the vision of Mr. B. have here given way to a newer, enlarged sensibility. Throughout the grounds everything flourishes—gardens, vineyard, the orangery—and content shows in the faces of the gardener and his wife, a veritable Darby and Joan standing in the door of their neat cottage. Sheep crop the lawns, and "alcoves, little temples, seats, are erected at different points of view." Throughout we see the happy balance between man and nature praised by Pope in his epistle to Burlington, a cooperation between ordering rationality and the untamed sublime.

Grandison Hall is to be a focus for social amity under its new owner. One of Sir Charles's first actions is to "break thro' the usual forms" (3:276) and invite all the neighborhood gentry to dinner. Everyone is so well entertained that they stay until six in the morning, Harriet reports, and "all was happy; and decency, good order, mirth and jollity, went thro' the whole space" (3:281). Nevertheless, it is the quiet gathering at home with family and close friends that is most typical of the Grandison circle. Harriet exclaims that she has found complete contentment: "The Domestic man, The cheerful Friend, The kind Master, The enlivening Companion, The polite Neighbour, the tender Husband! Let nobody who sees Sir Charles Grandison at home, say, that the private station is not that of true happiness" (3:281).

Sir Charles Grandison is, unfortunately, flawed by its intrinsic lack of emotional tension. Never was Johnson's well-known remark about Richardson, that if you read him for the story you would hang yourself, so well justified. The reader of *Grandison* must seek for other rewards and find pleasure in the fine discriminations of behavior and the minute gradations of moral perceptions that the more serene atmosphere of the novel makes possible. Charlotte, annoyed because her own conduct is criticized, asks Harriet whether a couple "so *studious* of obliging each other" may not "seem to confess that the matrimonial good understanding hangs by very slender thread?" (2:350). Harriet replies, "And do not the tenderest friendships . . . hang by *as* slender? Can delicate minds be united to each other but by delicate observances?" This exploration of delicate observances is the chief strength of the novel and undoubtedly the reason it was of so much interest to Austen and Eliot. For example, during their courtship Grandison is late for an engagement with Harriet and her family. Still sensitive about being a "second choice," and in what is for her an unusually touchy mood, she ponders the consequences of being linked to a man so "secure" that he is never discomposed, and envisions him asking "Whether I was *greatly* uneasy because of his absence?" (3:46). Her Uncle Selby teases her, increasing her discontent, but when Sir Charles does appear, not only is his delay completely explained but he tactfully addresses himself to everyone, and Harriet can happily report, "You see my dear, he made not apologies to me, as if he supposed *me* disappointed by his absence. I was afraid he would" (3:49).

Richardson's last novel, then, disappoints the expectations raised by *Clarissa* but offers instead an ideal picture of a world of moral sanity and humane behavior: a world that is made to seem possible if only every individual would follow the example of Sir Charles and act in a truly Christian way according to the powers that nature and his station in life have given him. *Grandison* rejects the false values of Clarissa's persecutors, both the hypocritical greed of the Harlowes and the sterile egotism of Lovelace, and offers the challenge of putting into practice the moral ideals to which that society so readily gave lip service. "Can he be so *very* good a man?," asks Harriet of Sir Charles, and answers, "What is in thy heart to doubt it? A fine reflection upon the age; as if there could not be *one* good man in it" (3:138).

Chapter Five
Reputation and Influence

From the first appearance of *Pamela,* Richardson's reception by literary critics was mixed, although the general reading public eagerly bought the book, and, indeed, almost anything connected with it. In 1741 there were nine works related to *Pamela* published in London, ranging from Fielding's satirical *Shamela* to a play by Henry Gifford, from a spurious continuation by John Kelly, to outright imitations such as *Memoires of the Life of Lady H—— the Celebrated Pamela.* This outpouring was certainly testimony to the great public interest in the novel and, in many cases, reflected a shrewd appreciation of the commercial possibilities of unauthorized "tie-ins." In the nineteenth century, in contrast, Richardson was generally relegated to a few paragraphs in literary histories where deference was paid to his pioneering role, but it was tactfully implied that no one except recondite scholars need actually read the novels. The twentieth century has seen a great revival of interest in Richardson, starting with the pioneering work of Alan McKillop in the 1930s and burgeoning at the present time. Richardson was fond of praise and, although diffident, hoped that his novels and his own reputation would live on. It is tempting to see him as a figure in the wings, watching as the chronicle of his critical fortunes unfolds, and to speculate about his reactions. Some of the laudatory judgments might seem as daunting to him as the detractions, but then, Richardson declared, "I always suspect Poetical Judges."[1]

The praise *Pamela* elicited tended to focus on its moral effects. The first notice of the novel appeared in the *Weekly Miscellany* in a letter addressed "To My Worthy Friend, the Author of Pamela," probably written by Richardson's friend William Webster, the editor of the periodical. The novel is praised for its moral instruction, and while stylistic features such as suspense and simplicity are admired, truthfulness is seen as the distinguishing characteristic. Such praise echoed Richardson's own aims, as expressed in his letter to Aaron Hill quoted above, which stressed "an easy and natural manner, suitably to the simplicity of it" producing "a new species of writing"that would "pro-

mote the cause of religion and virtue."[2] Richardson did indeed approve
of this first piece of criticism, and included it in the prefatory materials
to *Pamela*. The pro-*Pamela* forces continued to stress the truth to nature
found in the narrative, the simple appeal of its heroine, and the uplift-
ing moral message it conveyed.

Fielding was first in the field of the anti-*Pamela* forces with *Shamela*,
a devastating satire that attacked both the moral basis of the novel and
its style. In *Shamela,* as noted above, the heroine is seen as a hypocritical opportunist who leads the gullible Mr. B. on, scorning his offers
and pretending to guard her "vartue" but really keeping her eye on the
most lucrative prize of all—marriage. Fielding also struck a note of
class snobbery that would be echoed by other critics, declaring that
Pamela would instruct serving maids how to seduce their masters and
encourage young gentlemen to marry beneath them. The style of *Pamela* is parodied, with particular attention paid to its "low" diction and
to its use of detail, together with Richardson's method of "writing to
the moment" with the extensive use of the present tense. Fielding's
later novel *Joseph Andrews,* which begins as an amplified satire on Pamela, suggests by its deliberate stylization another criticism of Richardson's narrative mode. In *Joseph Andrews* we are immediately taken in
charge by an authoritative narrator who will begin each volume of the
novel with a prefatory note and who will not hesitate to suspend the
action of the story to digress on "high people and low people" or to
insert a "discourse between the poet and the player." Fielding insures
that the reader is reminded that this "History" is in fact a fiction and
that the story is artfully contrived. Richardson, on the other hand, hid
behind the mask of editor and preferred "that the *Air* of Genuineness"
should be maintained as if the narrative were an actual collection of
letters, "to avoid hurting that kind of Historical Faith which Fiction
itself is generally read with."[3] Fielding's radically different choice of
narrative method, his insistent emphasis on the presence of the author,
implies, perhaps, a criticism of Richardson's fictional mode that is parallel to his critique of Pamela's behavior. Just as Pamela, in Fielding's
view, hides behind a facade of prudery, so Richardson conceals himself
behind the pretense of an editor.

Other voices quickly joined the anti-*Pamela* forces, echoing Fielding's attack while stressing the impropriety of the "warm" scenes and
lamenting the novel's verbosity. *Clarissa* was much less controversial
than *Pamela,* and even Fielding generously joined in praising it, but
these two failings, impropriety and verbosity, were also ascribed to

Richardson's second novel. Richardson was sufficiently sensitive to the criticism of encouraging prurient interest to deal specifically with these attacks. In the sequel to *Pamela* Richardson, as described above, has Lady Davers declare that no right thinking reader of Pamela's account of her trials could take offense and that a certain amount of detail was necessary so that the limits of Mr. B.'s attempts are clearly understood. He replied to similar aspersions on *Clarissa* in his pamphlet "Answer to the Letter of a Very Reverend and Worthy Gentleman, Objecting to the Warmth of a Particular Scene in the 'History of Clarissa,' " but he was even more disturbed by the reaction of many readers, chiefly women, to his villain, Lovelace. These readers, clearly attracted to his rake, accused Clarissa of being prudish and pleaded with Richardson to reform Lovelace and end happily with a marriage. To counter this misreading of his characters Richardson added new material to the third edition, described as "Letters and Passages Restored from the Original Manuscripts of the 'History of Clarissa.' " (So that buyers of the original editions would not feel cheated, Richardson also published the new additions as a separate pamphlet.) These alterations all tended to blacken Lovelace's character and justify Clarissa's actions, often through the use of "editorial" intervention such as footnotes.[4] The charge of wordiness was to plague Richardson with *Sir Charles* as well, and in the postscript to *Clarissa* and the preface to *Sir Charles* he offers two somewhat conflicting justifications. He argues first that the method of "writing to the moment" inevitably makes the works lengthy but that it also makes them more lively, interesting, and affecting. Then, he notes that his books are intended not merely for the sake of entertainment, but for a nobler end, and that the story should be looked upon primarily as a vehicle of instruction. It is not stated, but certainly implied, that with this higher aim in mind the frivolous reader should be willing to forego the dubious pleasures of rapid turns of plot. The final declaration, however, is purely aesthetic, that "There is not one Episode in the Whole, nor . . . one Letter inserted but what tends to illustrate the principal Design." The assertion is made at the end of *Sir Charles Grandison,* but applies with even greater force to *Clarissa.*

Sir Charles Grandison was less popular than the two earlier novels. Praise was given, as before, for the book's exemplary portrayal of virtue, and the madness of Clementina was much admired, with the scenes compared favorably to Shakespeare's treatment of Ophelia. Sir Charles himself, coupled with the book's length, was pronounced dull and—in an objection that had also been raised about *Clarissa*—he was declared to be too perfect for verisimilitude. Richardson replied, in a concluding note, "that he performs no one action which it is not in the power of any man in his situation *to* perform" and went on to say that "it is surely both delightful and instructive to dwell sometimes on this bright side of things; To shew, by a series of facts in common life, what a degree of excellence may be attained and preserved amidst all the infection of fashionable vice and folly." A more serious objection, for Richardson, was criticism of Sir Charles's offer to allow his daughters to be raised as Roman Catholics in the event that he married Clementina, thereby showing less concern for female souls than for male. Richardson wrote a letter replying to this charge, printed as a free pamphlet, and later included in his *Collection of Sentiments*. The letter rehearses all of Sir Charles's problems with the Porettas and then explains that he was "in a manner *compelled*" to make some concessions, "in compassion to an excellent woman," but that "they are not countenanced by the *judgment* of Sir Charles Grandison," and makes clear that the offer is "by no means a precedent to be pleaded in *common* cases."[5]

A virtual compendium of contemporary English objections to Richardson appeared in a pamphlet, *Critical Remarks on "Sir Charles Grandison," "Clarissa" and "Pamela,"* by a "Lover of Virtue," published in 1754. The author finds *Clarissa*, on the whole, admirable although she is "rather too good."[6] *Pamela*, on the other hand, is not of a rank that would "entitle her to those notions of honour and virtue." *Sir Charles Grandison* is criticized for its lack of plot, and its hero has a benevolence that is too showy, contrasting unfavorably with Fielding's Allworthy. The writer is a freethinker and therefore finds Sir Charles unacceptable since he is supposed to be learned, yet has not become a skeptic. Above all, he accuses Richardson of encouraging indulgence in the passions and of therefore being responsible for "an infinite series of other compositions all of the same kind,"[7] written by imitators that promote a harmful and debilitating attitude. Richardson's use of coined words, the writer declares, has hastened the decline of the language. The epistolary style leads to intolerable length, and, it is suggested, Richardson pads his works to increase his profit as a printer.

On the Continent, Richardson's works were quickly translated, with varying degrees of accuracy, and, in general, met with an enthusiastic reception. A curious footnote to Richardson's success in Europe is the fact that he was one of the few English authors of the eighteenth century to be listed in the *Index,* the official Vatican list of prohibited books. Richardson himself apparently never knew of this, and, if he had, would undoubtedly have been dismayed, not only because of the implied criticism of the morality of his works, but also because he had been especially magnanimous himself in his treatment of the Roman Church in *Grandison.* Clementina's decision is lauded, and while the novel does question the theological basis of her acts, the firm belief in exclusive salvation that she espouses is accepted rather than ridiculed. The book that was actually placed on the *Index* was the French translation, by the Abbé Prévost, suggesting that the translator may have been the object of censure, rather than Richardson.

In Germany, in Holland, in France, and, indeed, on the entire Continent, *Pamela* became a vogue, and *Clarissa* quickly followed. While German critics were, in general, more sympathetic than French who sometimes found Richardson rather coarse and ill-suited to more refined tastes, undoubtedly both the most enthusiastic and the most influential critique was that of Diderot, written in 1761, the year of Richardson's death. In the eulogy Diderot declares that the term "novel" cannot justly be applied to the works of Richardson, because this label implies "a tissue of frivolous and imaginary events the perusal of which was dangerous to both taste and morals,"[8] whereas these works give us events "such as occur in every civilized nation of the world" and depict "the general tenor of the world just as I observe it all about me."[9] Furthermore, Richardson "draws your attention back to the important things in life" and, with his grasp of psychology, illuminates the mind, lighting up "the recesses of the cavern with his torch" so that we "discern those subtle and dishonest motives that hide deep within us."[10] Diderot places Richardson on a shelf with Moses, Homer, Euripides, and Sophocles, praises him for his ability to make readers identify with his characters, so that even oppressed virtue appears superior to triumphant vice, and notes that "his books have left a pleasing strain of melancholy in my character that does not fade."[11] The sentimental note struck by Diderot's last comment informed much of the continental vogue for Richardson, and, in the eyes of many commentators, suggests Richardson's characters as the genesis of young Werther and other figures of the romantic movement. European translations often expurgated, condensed, and even outright altered the novels, so in referring to "Richardson's influence" one may well be actually crediting works that were in themselves distorted reflections, and which gained popularity because they appealed to a taste that was already emerging from complex cultural forces. Certainly, to posit Richardson as a forefather to continental romanticism is to imply that he was, at best, only partially understood by his admirers. His influence on the European novel was nonetheless important, and can be traced through an outpouring of obviously imitative works such as Schulz's *Albertine,* published in 1788 and later reissued in 1797 as *Clarissa in Berlin,* as well as through more important works. Sarah Smith has pointed out that both Clarissa and Sir Charles, who adhere to their own moral code rather than bow to the conventions of society, encourage a model of "living to one's self," transcending worldly standards, that leads to the noble individuality of both the sentimental, quixotic hero and of the more assertive romantic rebel.

Richardson's influence on the English novel was also pervasive. The first and most obvious point to note is that after *Pamela* made fiction respectable other talents were attracted to the form. It is certainly arguable that Fielding would never have become a novelist if Richardson had never written. The opening up of this new literary genre as an acceptable medium of expression produced an explosion of talent, including Smollett and Sterne, and made the novel a dominant form in the nineteenth century. In tracing influence, the problem is, again, separating out themes that can be seen as emanating directly from the novels from similar tendencies that reflected diverse cultural trends. Since Richardson's works were seen as encouraging such contradictory ideas as sentimentalism, the romantic assertion of self, a doctrine of restraint, Puritan aversion to sexuality, interest in prurient detail, defense of neglected Christian values, and an undermining of the traditional bases of social order, trying to assess which novels were "Richardsonian" becomes a difficult task. The dedicated searcher can find traces of influence in a great number of works if that influence is defined broadly enough.

In terms of technique, if the contest is seen as Richardson versus Fielding, Fielding must be adjudged the winner. The epistolary novel did not survive into the next century as a popular form. Fielding's obtrusive and outspoken narrator was tempered down into the omniscient narrator, a convention that became the norm until the twentieth-century innovations of Joyce and Woolf. Richardson's focus, however, on the interior life of his characters was a pervasive influence. A kind of parlor game can be played, surveying the novels of the nineteenth century and declaring them "Richardsonian" or "Fieldingesque." Jane Austen is a case in point. Admirers of Fielding claim her as a descendant, pointing to her irony, her satiric tone, and her use of a wise narrator who sometimes offers guiding comments. On the other hand, her admiration of Richardson is well documented and recently scholars have offered evidence as to the direct parallels which can be pointed out between Austen's novels and those of Richardson, [12] where her characters echo his so closely as to suggest the possibility of deliberate reference. As the century goes on the influence of either Fielding or Richardson is further tempered by the work of other novelists, who themselves were undoubtedly influenced by these major figures, and the classification of writers becomes even more difficult and more tenuous. Certainly, even writers who had never read Richardson himself perceived the parameters of what constituted "the novel" in the light of the contributions he had made through his works.

Among critics, Richardson's reputation declined. A patronizing and denigrating tone comes to be present even when faint praise is being tendered. Since there was much in Richardson's work that could appeal to the romantic ethos and much also that could be thought of as consonant with Victorian morality, the pervasive depreciation is puzzling. It might be expected that romantics would be attracted by Richardson's portrayal of the individual upholding his own standards even if that ethic conflicts with the expectations of society. Clarissa and Lovelace are both potential fully romantic heroes in this sense, as is Pamela, although her standards represent at least a nominal or recognizable norm, and Sir Charles, who frequently asserts his readiness to act according to his own rather than society's code. The emotive or sentimental aspect of romanticism should have been delighted with Richardson's exploration of the "divided heart" and his method of involving his reader in the struggles of the protagonist, fostering empathetic participation in psychological struggle. The Victorian age, on the other hand, should have appreciated Richardson's not only moral but exemplary stance, which presents truly virtuous characters who, in the case of Pamela and, even more strikingly, Sir Charles, also exhibit a prudent grasp of the management of worldly concerns.

The prevalence of a different narrative style undoubtedly tended to make Richardson seem somewhat old-fashioned, a period piece. It is also true that as soon as Richardson became less fashionable, the length of *Clarissa,* his greatest work, became a problem. *Pamela* was more accessible simply because it was shorter. It also seems probable, however, that inferences from biography may have influenced Richardson's reputation. Even in 1958 R. F. Brissenden declared, "The character of

Richardson is an affront to every conception of what an artist should be."[13] When Brissenden explains that Richardson was "nothing but a middle-aged London printer, respected and prosperous, but in no way distinguished," it seems clear that he is using some postromantic formulation as to "what an artist should be." The romantics certainly would have been influenced negatively by Richardson's undeniably bourgeois life and by his business success. Boswell disliked Richardson and his picture of Richardson as vain, petty, and somehow not able to fit in with the masculine wits in whose company Boswell counted himself, further colored the age's picture of Richardson. It is a fact of literary history that once the critical climate turns against a work, an author, or a style, the effect becomes self-reinforcing until only the pronouncements of an authority of independent mind can reverse the trend. We tend to read as we are instructed to do so, and Richardson can be easily parodied or patronized, as Fielding demonstrated. The Victorians, who might have respected Richardson's strict morality, were probably influenced not only by the general agreement to damn with faint praise but also by a certain suspicion, in an era of vigorously masculine energy, of a man who was, according to biographical legend, constantly in the company of females.

The century starts well with Anna Letitia Barbauld's generally intelligent critique in *The British Novelists* (1810), which does at least take Richardson seriously and does basically approach him on his own terms. Coleridge, on the other hand, sees Richardson as a pernicious influence. In 1816, discussing the tragedy *Bertram,* written by Charles Robert Maturin, Coleridge digresses to examine the concept of "German Drama." He finds that this school is in fact thoroughly English, based upon German translations of Young's *Night Thoughts,* Harvey's *Meditations,* and Richardson's *Clarissa.* It is, he declares, a combination of the "bloated style" of Harvey, the "strained thoughts, the figurative metaphysics, and solemn epigrams" of Young and "the loaded sensibility, the minute detail, the morbid consciousness of every thought and feeling in the whole flux and reflux of the mind, in short the self-involution and dreamlike continuity of Richardson."[14] Coleridge has indeed perceived some of the salient characteristics of Richardson's work, but finds it contributing to a genre "denounced, by the best critics in Germany, as the mere cramps of weakness, and orgasms of a sickly imagination on the part of the author, and the lowest provocation of torpid feeling on that of the readers."[15]

Hazlitt, in a series of lectures delivered in 1818, gives Fielding and

Smollett primacy of place and then turns to Richardson. He finds him difficult to classify since, in contrast to the first two novelists, he is neither an observer of human life nor a describer of its eccentricities, but one "who seemed to spin his materials entirely out of his own brain, as if there has been nothing existing in the world beyond the little shop in which he sat writing."[16] The gratuitous inclusion of "the little shop"—hardly an adequate description of the milieu of one of London's leading printers—indicates, perhaps, the bias against "bourgeois" Richardson discussed above. Hazlitt finds "an artificial reality" in Richardson's works and is puzzled by the mingling of "the romantic air of pure fiction, with the literal minuteness of a common diary."[17] He finds the novels to be "an anomaly in the history of human genius."[18] While Hazlitt then finds much to admire in the novels—every circumstance is made to tell, the exactness of detail gives an appearance of truth, we feel that we are introduced into a large family, and Richardson's powers of invention are prodigious—the impression that Richardson is a "period piece" colors the discussion.

In assessing *Pamela,* Hazlitt praises the development of the character, noting that "her sentiments gradually expand themselves, . . . she writes better every time . . . just as a girl would do, writing such letters in such circumstances" and then undercuts this by the italicized "and yet it is certain *that no girl would write such letters in such circumstances.*"[19] He finds that "if the business of life consisted in letter-writing . . . human nature would be what Richardson represents it." Hazlitt declares that Richardson's medium, the letter, which permits "a careful review of every motive and circumstance," results in feelings being "blunted and deadened by being presented through a medium which may be true to reason, but is false in nature."[20] Hazlitt, clearly, is reading Richardson's work in a way completely opposite to what Richardson intended, and it seems valid to infer that the choice of an epistolary style had become, by 1818, a real stumbling block in reading the novels. Hazlitt complains that Richardson's style gives "an appearance of coldness and formality" to his characters and that "every thing is too conscious in his works," although he also praises, somewhat contradictorily, the fact that "every thing is brought home in its full force to the mind of the reader."[21] He praises Clarissa in terms that show he was also sympathetic to Lovelace: "she who could triumph by her virtue, and the force of her love, over the regality of Lovelace's mind, his wit, his person, his accomplishments and his spirit, conquers all hearts."[22] And, with perhaps a note of incredulity, Hazlitt acknowledges that "with a boldness greater even than his puritanical severity, [Richardson] has exhausted every topic on virtue and vice."[23] Hazlitt's consideration of Richardson concludes with *Grandison,* denigrating "the little, selfish, affected, insignificant Miss Byron" in comparison with "the divine Clementina," and declaring that "Sir Charles is the prince of coxcombs" so that "there is nothing which excites so little sympathy as his excessive egotism."[24]

Scott's *Lives of the Novelists,* originally published as prefaces to a collection, Ballantyne's *Novelist's Library,* in 1821, begins the discussion of Richardson by giving credit to Mrs. Barbauld, who has written the "life of this excellent man, and ingenious author . . . with equal spirit and candour," [25] and, after praising him as "the mild good man which we could wish to suppose him," observes that vanity was Richardson's greatest failing, and notes that he was "peculiarly susceptible of this feminine weakness" because of the gentleness of his mind. Scott observes that "there seems to have been a want of masculine firmness in Richardson's habits of thinking" and notes, disapprovingly, that this led him "to prefer the society of women."[26] Scott quotes Boswell to support his view. Both the character of Pamela, as depicting "the pure and modest character of an English maiden," and the presentation of it which expresses "those thoughts and reasons exactly as she must have done had the fictitious incident really befallen such a person,"[27] are praised, although Scott questions whether the plot may not encourage "rash enterprise" rather than "virtuous resistance."[28]

Scott is even more pleased with *Clarissa,* admiring the heroine as perfection and finding Lovelace a character of rare balance who attracts the reader by his wit but repels him through his villainy. Clarissa is seen as truly heroic, showing that "there is a chastity of the soul" and rejecting all offers of marriage even though "a common mind" might have accepted "as a refuge against worldly dishonor."[29] Scott perceives that Lovelace can never be a suitable husband—"his mind is too perverted, his imagination too much inflamed . . . , his heart is too much hardened."[30] The distinction of *Clarissa,* Scott declares, is that "No work had appeared before, perhaps none has appeared since containing so many direct appeals to the passions, stated too in a manner so irresistible."[31]

Grandison, on the other hand, Scott finds inferior. The hero is "a faultless monster,"[32] Harriet Byron is indelicate, the only character in whom the reader can take a real interest is Clementina. Richardson, nevertheless, will be credited with being the first "who threw aside the trappings of romance, with all its extravagance, and appealed to the genuine passions of the human heart."[33] Scott praises Richardson's new style of writing, but finds Johnson's preference of Richardson over Fielding too high. Scott modifies Johnson's famous comparison of Richardson being like a man who knew how the watch was made, while Fielding was one who could tell the hour by looking at the dial, to both being "excellent mechanics," the difference being that Richardson's time pieces showed "a great deal of the internal work by which the index is regulated; while those of Fielding merely point to the hour of the day, being all that most men desire to know," and continuing with a still more disparaging analogy that Fielding's works are like "free, bold, and true sketches" while Richardson's are like paintings "minutely laboured" which, however excellent, "exhibit . . . heaviness."[34] Scott concludes by noting that while no "collection" would be complete without the novels of Richardson, he is now much neglected and his final judgment places Richardson firmly in the past perfect: "Yet under all these disadvantages, the genius of Richardson must ever be acknowledged to have done honour to the language in which he wrote, and his . . . talents to have been of service to morality."[35]

In *The English Humourists* Thackeray wastes no time launching into comparisons between Richardson and Fielding, finding the latter's "hearty contempt and antipathy" to *Pamela* entirely understandable. He declares that Fielding could hardly "do otherwise than laugh at the puny cockney bookseller" and that it was natural to "hold him up to scorn as a mollcoddle and a milksop" for "pouring out endless volumes of sentimental twaddle."[36] Whereas Fielding's muse "had sung the loudest in tavern choruses," Richardson's goddess "was attended by old maids and dowagers."[37] Acknowledging Johnson's preference of Richardson, Thackeray proudly declares that "a greater scholar than Johnson" admired Fielding, and cites this quotation from Gibbon: "Our immortal Fielding was of the younger branch of the Earls of Denbigh, who drew their origin from the Counts of Hapsburgh. The successors of Charles V may distain their brethren of England, but the romance of 'Tom Jones,' that exquisite picture of humour and manners, will outlive the palace of the Escurial and the Imperial Eagle of Austria." He underlines the significance of this curious blend of snobbery and chauvinism by adding, "There can be no gainsaying the sentence of this great judge. To have your name mentioned by Gibbon, is like having it written on the dome of St. Peters."[38] Johnson, on the other hand, is dismissed as being indebted to Richardson as a kind friend.

The tone of these nineteenth-century assessments carried over into the twentieth. George Saintsbury's *The English Novel,* first published in 1913, was both influential and typical. He sums up a very brief biographical account of the major novelists by finding Richardson "a respectable person of rather feminine temperament" who, "though good-natured to his friends," was "endowed with a feminine spitefulness." Fielding, on the other hand, while perhaps reckless and disorderly, "appears to have been in the main a thorough gentleman."[39] The very appearance of *Pamela,* in Saintsbury's eyes, deserves to be included in "the long 'history of the Unexpected,' " which "thick-strewn as it is with curiosities" can scarcely exhibit "anything odder,"[40] and he even suggests that Richardson's occupation as a printer was fortuitous since his own work could not encounter obstacles to publication that "frequently beset the appearance of greater works."

Pamela is praised chiefly for the lively unfolding of the story "in a sort of rapid dance . . . which is inspiriting and contagious."[41] The characters are dismissed as adequate but not first class. Pamela is praised as probable, but not reaching "the last triumph of originality and individuality,"[42] remaining an admirably worked out stereotype. Saintsbury disapproves of the letter convention, finding it artificial and tending toward length and verbosity, although he does concede that it allows opportunity for "Richardson's own special and peculiar gift of minute analysis of mood, temper and motive,"[43] "a gift that Saintsbury then undercuts by remarking, "but analysis for analysis' sake can have few real, though it may have some pretended, devotees."[44]

Saintsbury excuses himself from dealing at any length with Richardson's other novels, noting, with an implicit sigh of relief, that his subject is the history of the English novel, and that *Pamela* must therefore be given some importance, but the historically subordinate books can be dispensed with quickly. *Clarissa* is characterized as "a sort of enlarged, diversified, and transposed *Pamela.*"[45] While Clarissa herself has generally aroused compassion, Saintsbury finds her unsympathetic—prudish, proud, devious, she lacks passion and "one's pity for her never comes very near to love."[46] He also denigrates the currently orthodox attitude of shocked admiration of Lovelace, finding that "he is not in the least a gentleman except in externals, and there is nothing really 'great' about him at all."[47] Grandison, not unexpectedly, is pronounced a "faultless and insufferable monster."[48] In summing up, Saintsbury gives Richardson credit for "gathering up the scattered means and methods which had been half ignorantly hit on by others," for using an "elaborate 'minor psychology' as it may be called," and for catching the attention of his readers. He excuses the "unhealthiness of atmosphere" as not just "the result of imperfect temperament and breeding" but also as "closely connected with his very method." Finally, Saintsbury makes the judgment that "the greatest of Richardson's works is his successor, caricaturist, and superior—Fielding,"[49] who is praised for his "genial, wholesome, and, above all, masculine taste and intellect." Narrative method, characterization, description, are here all superior, and, "in short, Fielding used his reluctant and indignant forerunner as a spring-board, whence to attain heights which that forerunner could never have reached."[50] Fielding was "to discard all kinds of adventitious aids" and go "his own way—and the Way of the Novel."[51] Richardson is thus relegated to a necessary footnote in the history of the novel, whose claim even to originality is dubious, and who is quickly superseded in every way by Fielding. Saintsbury's view reflected the norm in the early twentieth century. Richardson was patronizingly cited as a rather tedious primitive, and probably very little read. Here again Richardson was not aided by the fact that *Pamela* was the one work serious students felt they should read as "the first English novel" whereas *Clarissa,* his greatest but also longest work, they felt quite comfortable ignoring. An analogous misjudgment would result if the literary establishment were to read only Shakespeare's early comedies and never turn to the mature tragedies.

The modern view of Richardson is based upon the works of two major Richardson scholars, Alan Dugald McKillop and William M. Sale, both published in 1936. Sale's *Samuel Richardson: A Bibliographical Record of His Literary Career with Historical Notes*[52] which was followed by *Samuel Richardson: Master Printer* in 1950,[53] provided a descriptive bibliography of Richardson's works and of works inspired by the novels. The later book gives a picture of Richardson as a printer, with details about his practices as an employer, government contracts, relations with the trade, and the general milieu of Fleet Street in his time. A list of books printed by Richardson is appended, together with a catalog of printer's ornaments used by Richardson. Sale's work is invaluable not only in identifying Richardson's own more obscure writings but in showing the range of works that passed through his hands and giving a clear picture of Richardson as an important figure in the London publishing world, a correction to Hazlitt's picture of the "little shop." McKillop's work, *Samuel Richardson, Printer and Novelist,*[54] was a seminal study that took Richardson seriously as a literary artist, examining the novels in sympathetic detail and placing them in a historical context. McKillop made extensive use of Richardson's correspondence to trace the development of the novels and to document Richardson's artistic discussions with his circle of admirers. Noting that "a common view of Richardson's work in fiction is that he was an interminable blunderer who, without understanding what he was doing, developed certain characters and situations which hit the taste of his day and which still have some interest for the historically minded,"[55] McKillop asserts that "it is impossible to fit *Clarissa* into any such scheme." He sees *Clarissa* as "a remarkably bold and independent piece of work,"[56] and explores Richardson's "characteristic method of elaborate analysis of a situation by a record of mood, reflection, dialogue and gesture."[57] McKillop's work made impossible the automatic response to Richardson as one of patronizing denigration.

The 1950s saw the publication of a number of works that explored different aspects of Richardson's achievement. Northrup Frye described Richardson's technique as an art of "process"[58] while Dorothy Van Ghent posited a psychological reading of *Clarissa* in which Richardson unconsciously creates a Protestant myth.[59] Ian Watt's *The Rise of the Novel*[60] treated *Pamela* and *Clarissa* in the context of sociological change, seeing Richardson as a spokesman for his urban and bourgeois society.

Interest in Richardson has continued to increase. In 1971 T. C. Duncan Eaves and Ben D. Kimpel published an authoritative biography,[61] while Richard Hannaford in 1980,[62] and Sarah Smith in 1984[63] have each produced excellent bibliographies, all of great value to the Richardson scholar. Hannaford suggests that works since 1971 have the character of "second-generation"[64] criticism, based on the assumption both of Richardson's conscious artistry and of his aesthetic significance, and redirecting the reader's attention to the real Richardson. The major works of this period, listed in the bibliography, consider the novels in the light of Puritan attitudes, psychological theories, dramatic techniques, emblematic imagery, conscious craftsmanship, Marxism, feminism, and, most recently, poststructuralist critical methods.

The direction scholarship will take in the future is risky to predict, but it can be confidently asserted that the work of the last fifty years has assured Richardson of a reputation as a major novelist, rather than merely a historical oddity. While it was once customary to decry his narrow Puritan code, readers now see a humanistic insistence on the integrity of the individual, and especially of women, as Richardson shows characters contending with a society that hypocritically ignores in action the values it proclaims in words. While formerly his exemplars were pronounced stereotypes, credit is now given to Richardson as the originator of psychological realism. While he was often patronized as a bumbler who achieved his best effects without, or even contrary to, his conscious intentions, he is now admired as a masterly craftsman, and the exploration of his literary techniques is still yielding new discoveries. Richardson has been fully reinstated in the position of "Father of the English Novel" not only historically, but as an important figure for the study of fictional theory and technique as well as the author of one of the greatest novels ever written.

Notes and References

Chapter One

1. William Sale, Jr., *Samuel Richardson: Master Printer* (Ithaca: Cornell University Press, 1950), 17.
2. T. C. Duncan Eaves and Ben D. Kimpel, *Samuel Richardson: A Biography* (Oxford, Clarendon Press, 1971).
3. Ibid., 5.
4. See William C. Slattery, *The Richardson-Stinstra Correspondence* (Carbondale: Southern Illinois University Press, 1969), and John Carroll, *Selected Letters of Samuel Richardson* (Oxford: Clarendon Press, 1964).
5. Slattery, *Richardson-Stinstra Correspondence,* 24; Carroll, *Selected Letters,* 229.
6. Ibid.
7. Allyn Reade, "Samuel Richardson and His Family Circle," *Notes & Queries,* 12th ser., (1922):182.
8. Slattery, *Richardson-Stinstra Correspondence,* 24–25; Carroll, *Selected Letters,* 229.
9. Eaves and Kimpel, *Samuel Richardson,* 11.
10. Carroll, *Selected Letters,* 109.
11. Forster MSS, XI, f. 259, 5 June 1959, Victoria and Albert Museum, London.
12. Carroll, *Selected Letters,* 193.
13. Ibid.
14. Ibid, 323.
15. MSS at the Pierpont Morgan Library.
16. R. F. Brissenden, *Samuel Richardson* (London: Longmans, Green 1958), 9.
17. James Boswell, *The Life of Samuel Johnson,* ed. George Birkbeck Hill and L. F. Powell (Oxford: Clarendon Press, 1934), 2:48–49, 174–75.
18. Ibid., 3:314.
19. Ibid., 1:145-47.
20. Eaves and Kimpel, *Samuel Richardson,* 334.
21. For the evidence see Elizabeth Bergen Brophy, *Samuel Richardson: The Triumph of Craft* (Knoxville: University of Tennessee Press, 1974), 113–115.
22. Carroll, *Selected Letters,* 230; Slattery, *Richardson-Stinstra Correspondence,* 26; Alan McKillop, *The Early Masters of English Fiction* (Lawrence: University of Kansas Press, 1956), 47–51.

23. Carroll, *Selected Letters*, 231; Slattery, *Richardson-Stinstra Correspondence*, 27; McKillop, *English Fiction*, 49.

24. Carroll, *Selected Letters*, 230; Slattery, *Richardson-Stinstra Correspondence*, 27; McKillop, *English Fiction*, 48.

25. For the extent of Richardson's involvement in these revisions see Eaves and Kimpel, *Samuel Richardson*, 72, n. 56.

26. See Alan Dugald McKillop, "Richardson's Early Writings: Another Pamphlet," *Journal of English and Germanic Philology*, 53 (1954):72–75, and Eaves and Kimpel, *Samuel Richardson*, 54.

27. For a more complete discussion of Richardson's revisions see Katherine Hornbeak, "Richardson's Familiar Letters and the Domestic Conduct Books: Richardson's Aesop, *Smith College Studies in Modern Languages* 19, no. 2 (1938):30–50, and Eaves and Kimpel, *Samuel Richardson*, 76–80.

28. Eaves and Kimpel, *Samuel Richardson*, 79.

29. British Library Add. MS 6190, f. 32.

30. For a discussion, see Eaves and Kimpel, *Samuel Richardson*, 82.

31. Slattery, *Richardson-Stinstra Correspondence*, 28; Carroll, *Selected Letters*, 232.

32. Hornbeak, "Richardson's Familiar Letters," 104.

33. *Familiar Letters on Important Occasions*, ed. Brian Downs (London: Routledge, 1928), 46; hereafter cited in the text.

34. See Alan D. McKillop, "Richardson, Young, and the *Conjectures*," *Modern Philology* 22 (1925):391–404.

35. See Eaves and Kimpel, *Samuel Richardson*, 498.

Chapter Two

1. See John Richetti, *Prose Fiction before Richardson* (Oxford: Clarendon Press, 1969) 9.

2. Carroll, *Selected Letters*, 41.

3. Samuel Johnson, *The Rambler* (New Haven: Yale University Press, 1969), 24.

4. Samuel Richardson, *Pamela* (London: Dent, 1962) 1; hereafter cited in the text. *Pamela* in this discussion refers to the original novel, contained in the above. Richardson's sequel, which will be discussed later, will be referred to as *Pamela II* (London: Dent, 1962).

5. Carroll, *Selected Letters*, 329.

6. Samuel Richardson, *Clarissa, Preface, Hints of Prefaces, and Postscript*, ed. R. F. Brissenden (Los Angeles: University of California Press 1964), 6.

7. Carroll, *Selected Letters*, 157.

8. *The Complete Letters of Lady Mary Wortley Montagu*, ed. Robert Halsband (Oxford: Clarendon Press, 1967), 3:90.

9. Samuel Richardson, *A Collection of the Moral and Instructive Senti-*

ments . . . in the Histories of Pamela, Clarissa and Sir Charles Grandison (London, 1755), 408.

10. Henry Fielding, *An Apology for the Life of Mrs. Shamela Andrews,* ed. Martin Battestin (Boston: Houghton Mifflin Co., 1961), 311.

11. Carroll, *Selected Letters,* 289.

12. Ibid., 315.

13. Ibid., 47.

14. Joseph Addison and Richard Steele, *The Spectator,* ed. Donald F. Bond (Oxford: Clarendon Press, 1965), 1:13.

15. Carroll, *Selected Letters,* 85.

16. See Eaves and Kimpel, *Samuel Richardson,* 127–34.

17. Carroll, *Selected Letters,* 43–44.

18. Ibid., 45.

Chapter Three

1. See Eaves and Kimpel, *Samuel Richardson,* 205–13.

2. Christina Marsden Gillis, *The Paradox of Privacy: Epistolary Form in Clarissa* (Gainesville: University Presses of Florida, 1984).

3. Carroll, *Selected Letters,* 296.

4. Ibid., 315.

5. Ibid., 296. For the reading "Carvers" for Carroll's "Carpers" (asterisked as doubtful) see Elizabeth Bergen Brophy, "A Richardson Letter: 'Carpers' or 'Carvers'?" *Notes and Queries,* February 1978, 44–45.

6. Samuel Richardson, *Clarissa,* 4 vols. (London: Dent, 1962), 1:53; hereafter cited in the text.

7. Carroll, *Selected Letters,* 92.

8. Mark Kinkead-Weekes, *Samuel Richardson: Dramatic Novelist* (Ithaca: Cornell University Press, 1973), 237.

9. I have here somewhat altered the position I took earlier in *Samuel Richardson,* 105–6.

10. Carroll, *Selected Letters,* 110.

11. Ian Watt, *The Rise of the Novel* (Berkeley: University of California Press, 1965), 145.

12. Cynthia Griffin Wolff, *Samuel Richardson and the Eighteenth-Century Puritan Character* (Hamden: Archon, 1972), 248.

13. Gillis, *Paradox of Privacy,* 50–52.

14. Kinkead-Weekes, *Samuel Richardson,* 241.

15. Terry Castle, *Clarissa's Ciphers* (Ithaca: Cornell University Press, 1982).

16. *Letters of Samuel Johnson,* ed. R. W. Chapman (Oxford: Clarendon, 1952) 1:54.

17. Boswell, *Life of Johnson,* 2:48–49.

Chapter Four

    1. Carroll, *Selected Letters,* 133.

    2. Ibid., 127.

    3. Ibid., 175

    4. Ibid., 127.

    5. Ibid., 179.

    6. *The History of Sir Charles Grandison* (London: Oxford University Press, 1972), 2:313; hereafter cited in the text.

    7. Carroll, *Selected Letters,* 133.

    8. Ibid., 161.

    9. Ibid., 168.

    10. Ibid., 315.

    11. Ibid., 186.

    12. Ibid., 286.

    13. Ibid., 179–80.

    14. Ibid., 218.

    15. J. E. Austen Leigh, *Memoir of Jane Austen,* ed. R. W. Chapman (1926), 89; cited in *Grandison,* xxiii.

    16. To Sara Sophia Hennell, 13 October 1847; *The George Eliot Letters,* 1:240; cited in *Grandison,* xxiii.

    17. See Watt, *Rise of the Novel,* 144–48.

    18. Others, notably Mary Astell in *A Serious Proposal to the Ladies* (1694), had proposed such establishments as a useful refuge for spinsters.

    19. I here echo the terminology used by Kinkead-Weekes in his discussion of *Grandison* as including two narratives, one a novel of "Ought" and the other of "Is."

    20. Richardson himself was a very generous man, continuing throughout his life a series of private personal charities. He estimated that he had given away a sum equal to his remaining estate. See Eaves and Kimpel, *Samuel Richardson,* 532.

    21. Pope's *Essay on Man,* especially epistles 2 and 3, is the best-known literary expression of the doctrine.

Chapter Five

    1. Carroll, *Selected Letters,* 271.

    2. Ibid., 41.

    3. Ibid., 85.

    4. See M. Kinkead-Weekes, "*Clarissa* Restored," *Review of English Studies* 10 (1959):156–71.

    5. *Grandison,* 3:473.

    6. *Critical Remarks on "Sir Charles Grandison," "Clarissa" and "Pamela,"* (Los Angeles, 1950), 24.

7. Ibid., 4.

8. *Diderot's Selected Writings,* ed. Lester G. Crocker, trans. Derek Colt-man (New York: Macmillan, 1966), 108.

9. Ibid., 109.

10. Ibid., 110.

11. Ibid.,111.

12. Papers read at 12th Annual Meeting of ASECS, April 1981: Jocelyn Harris, "Pride, Prejudice and *Grandison*"; Sarah Smith, "Words of Wisdom: Moral Style in Richardson and Austen."

13. Brissenden, *Samuel Richardson,* 9.

14. Samuel Taylor Coleridge, *The Collected Works of Samuel Taylor Coleridge,* vol. 7, *Biographia Literaria,* vol. 2 (Princeton: Princeton University Press, 1983), 211.

15. Ibid., 7, II, 211. The editors note that "orgasm" is not used in the sense common now but as in *O.E.D.* 1 ("Immoderate or violent excitement; rage, fury").

16. *The Complete Works of William Hazlitt,* ed. P. P. Howe (London: J. M. Dent, 1933), 16, 15.

17. Ibid., 15.

18. Ibid., 16.

19. Ibid., 17.

20. Ibid.

21. Ibid.

22. Ibid., 18.

23. Ibid.

24. Ibid.

25. Walter Scott, *Lives of the Novelists,* intro. George Saintsbury, (London: J. M. Dent, 1928), 1.

26. Ibid., 7.

27. Ibid., 21.

28. Ibid., 20.

29. Ibid., 25.

30. Ibid., 27.

31. Ibid., 29.

32. Ibid., 32.

33. Ibid., 39.

34. Ibid., 34.

35. Ibid., 35.

36. *The Works of William Makepeace Thackeray* (London: Smith, Elder & Co., 1911), 11:301–2.

37. Ibid., 302.

38. Ibid., 303.

39. George Saintsbury, *The English Novel* (London: J. M. Dent, 1927), 81.

40. Ibid., 82.

41. Ibid., 85.

42. Ibid., 87.

43. Ibid., 91.

44. Ibid., 93.

45. Ibid., 94.

46. Ibid., 95.

47. Ibid., 96.

48. Ibid., 94.

49. Ibid., 98.

50. Ibid., 102.

51. Ibid., 105.

52. William M. Sale, Jr., *Samuel Richardson: A Bibliographical Record of his Literary Career* (Hamden, Conn.: Archon Books, 1969).

53. Sale, *Samuel Richardson: Master Printer.*

54. Alan Dugald McKillop, *Samuel Richardson, Printer and Novelist* (Chapel Hill: University of North Carolina Press, 1936), 107.

55. Ibid., 107.

56. Ibid., 136.

57. Ibid., 154.

58. Northrup Frye, "Towards Defining an Age of Sensibility," *English Literary History* 23. (1956):144–52.

59. Dorothy Van Ghent, *The English Novel: Form and Function* (New York: Rinehart & Co. 1953).

60. Watt, *Rise of the Novel.*

61. Eaves and Kimpel, *Samuel Richardson.*

62. Richard Hannaford, *Samuel Richardson: An Annotated Bibliography of Critical Studies* (New York: Garland, 1980).

63. Sarah Smith, *Samuel Richardson: A Reference Guide* (Boston: Hall, 1984).

64. Hannaford, *Samuel Richardson,* xviii.

Selected Bibliography

PRIMARY SOURCES

1. Novels

The Novels of Samuel Richardson. Shakespeare Head Edition. 18 vols. Oxford, 1929–31. This edition, long out of print, used to be considered the standard edition and is often cited by scholars.

Clarissa. Everyman's Library. 4 vols. London: J. M. Dent & Sons, 1962. Long the only complete edition in print, this is currently cited by most scholars.

Clarissa. London: Penguin Books, 1986. Edited by Angus Ross, this is a scholarly edition based upon Richardson's first edition of 1747.

Pamela. Everyman's Library. 2 vols. London: J. M. Dent & Sons, 1962. The only edition in print that includes the continuation, *Pamela II.*

Pamela. Boston: Houghton Mifflin, 1971. Edited by Eaves and Kimpel, this follows the first edition of the novel.

Pamela. London: Penguin Books, 1982. Edited by Peter Sabor, this follows Richardson's final revisions of the novel, not published until 1804.

Sir Charles Grandison. 3 vols. Oxford: Oxford University Press, 1972. An excellent scholarly edition edited by Jocelyn Harris.

2. Miscellaneous Works

The Apprentice's Vade Mecum (1734). Edited by Alan Dugald McKillop. Los Angeles: University of California, William Andrews Clark Memorial Library, 1975.

Clarissa, Preface, Hints of Prefaces, and Postscript. Edited by R. F. Brissenden. Los Angeles: University of California, William Andrews Clark Memorial Library, 1964.

Familiar Letters on Important Occasions. Edited by Brian Downs. London: Routledge, 1928.

A Letter from Samuel Richardson, Esq. formerly a Member of the Company of Stationers and Given by Them to the Youths Bound at Their Hall. London: Stationer's Hall, n.d.

Samuel Richardson's Introduction to Pamela. Edited by Sheridan Baker, Jr. Los Angeles: University of California, William Andrews Clark Memorial Library, 1948.

3. Correspondence

The Correspondence of Samuel Richardson. Edited by Anna Laetitia Barbauld. 6
     vols. London: Lewis & Roden, 1804. Incomplete but still valuable since
     it prints some letters that have since disappeared.
Selected Letters of Samuel Richardson. Edited by John Carroll. Oxford: Clarendon
     Press, 1964.
The Richardson-Stinstra Correspondence, Edited by William Slattery. Carbondale:
     Southern Illinois University Press, 1969.

SECONDARY SOURCES

1. Bibliographies

Hannaford, Richard Gordon. *Samuel Richardson: An Annotated Bibliography of
     Critical Studies.* New York: Garland Publishing, 1980.
Sale, William M., Jr. *Samuel Richardson: A Bibliographical Record of His Literary
     Career with Historical Notes.* 1936. Reprint. Hamden, Conn.: Archon
     Books, 1969.
Smith, Sarah W. R. *Samuel Richardson: A Reference Guide.* Boston: G. K. Hall,
     1984.

2. Biography

Eaves, T. C. Duncan, and Kimpel, Ben D. *Samuel Richardson: A Biography.*
     Oxford: Clarendon Press, 1971. The standard authoritative biography.
     Includes a list of all known letters, and critical discussions of the works.
Sale, William M., Jr. *Samuel Richardson: Master Printer.* Ithaca, New York:
     Cornell University Press, 1950. A detailed account of Richardson's career
     as a printer, including lists of books known to be printed by Richardson.

3. Books

Brophy, Elizabeth B. *Samuel Richardson: the Triumph of Craft.* Knoxville: Uni-
     versity of Tennessee Press, 1974. A formulation of Richardson's artistic
     precepts and an analysis of the novels in the light of those precepts.
Castle, Terry. *Clarissa's Ciphers.* Ithaca: Cornell University Press, 1982. Draw-
     ing on recent hermeneutic theory, as well as feminist criticism, this work
     explicates the way in which the characters of the novel are engaged in a
     continual process of interpretation, trying to impose meaning on others.
Doody, Margaret Anne. *A Natural Passion: A Study of the Novels of Samuel
     Richardson.* Oxford: Clarendon Press, 1974. A discussion of the achieve-
     ment of the novels in relation to sources and analogues, but with special
     emphasis upon visual imagery.
Flynn, Carol Houlihan. *Samuel Richardson: A Man of Letters.* Princeton: Prince-
     ton University Press, 1982. Explores the images of the sentimental

woman, the fallen woman, and the rake in Richardson's novels and posits that by speaking through his characters Richardson invented a bolder, freer personality for himself.

Gillis, Christina Marsden. *The Paradox of Privacy: Epistolary Form in Clarissa.* Gainsville: University Presses of Florida, 1984. Examines Richardson's use of space and enclosure in *Clarissa* together with his recognition of the ambiguities of the letter form.

Goldberg, Rita. *Sex and Enlightenment: Women in Richardson & Diderot.* Cambridge: Cambridge University Press, 1984. Considers *Clarissa* against the background of European and Puritan thought, arguing that Richardson's work had a revolutionary impact on the "feminization of culture."

Golden, Morris. *Richardson's Characters.* Ann Arbor: University of Michigan Press, 1963. Richardson's characters are seen as the embodiment of fantasies, primarily of control and domination.

Hornbeak, Katherine G. "Richardson's Familiar Letters and the Domestic Conduct Books." *Smith College Studies in Modern Languages* 19, (1934). Demonstrates that Richardson's work is closer in spirit to domestic conduct books than to the usual letter writing manuals.

Kinkead-Weekes, Mark. *Samuel Richardson: Dramatic Novelist.* Ithaca: Cornell University Press, 1973. A detailed explication of the novels that follows them "from situation to situation, exploring the implications of each in a flexible, changing and complex process." Defends Richardson as a conscious artist who pioneered the narrative mode of writing from different points of view.

Konigsberg, Ira. *Samuel Richardson and the Dramatic Novel.* Lexington: University of Kentucky Press, 1968. Argues that Richardson used both the subject matter and techniques of drama, combining them with earlier fictional modes to produce a new form.

McKillop, Alan Dugald. *Samuel Richardson, Printer and Novelist.* 1936. Reprint. Hamden, Conn.: Shoe String Press, 1960. A pioneering study of Richardson. Assesses his achievement as a novelist and describes his milieu, his reputation and influence.

———. *The Early Masters of English Fiction.* Lawrence: University Press of Kansas, 1968. The section on Richardson offers a lucid discussion of the three novels.

Van Ghent, Dorothy. *The English Novel: Form and Function.* 1953. Reprint. New York: Holt, Rinehart & Winston, 1964. The chapter on *Clarissa* explores the images and symbols of the novels through modern psychology and suggests a mythic meaning.

Watt, Ian. *The Rise of the Novel: Studies in Defoe, Richardson and Fielding.* 1957. Reprint. Berkeley: University of California Press, 1971. An important study of the early novel stressing the social background. Chapters on *Pamela* and *Clarissa.*

Warner, William Beatty. *Reading Clarissa: The Struggles of Interpretation.* New

Haven: Yale University Press, 1979. This poststructuralist study of *Clarissa* proposes Lovelace as hero, finding most readings of the novel by "humanist" critics distorted because they have been conned into belonging "to Clarissa's party."

Wolff, Cynthia Griffin. *Samuel Richardson and the Eighteenth-Century Puritan Character.* Hamden, Conn.: Archon Books, 1972. Primarily a psychological study that explores the novels against the background of Puritan thought.

4. Articles

Dussinger, John A. "What Pamela Knew: An Interpretation." *Journal of English and Germanic Philology* 69 (1970):377–93. Discusses how Richardson's method subtly discloses the development of Pamela's subjective reality, allowing the reader to follow her perceptions through the stages of the narrative.

Frye, Northrup. "Towards Defining an Age of Sensibility." *English Literary History* 23 (1956). 144–52. Examines Richardson's method as an art of "process," a kind of narrative suitable for an age that emphasized the personal and biographical.

Hill, Christopher. "Clarissa Harlowe and her Times." *Essays in Criticism* 5 (1955):315–40. A standard explication of the historical and economic background of the novel.

Index

135